DREAMS 2 DESTINY

INTERACTIVE STUDY COURSE

DREAMS 2 DESTINY

INTERACTIVE STUDY COURSE

Identify Your Gifts & Talents,
Realize Your Life Calling,
Find True Fulfillment

by

Joseph S. Jones

Harrison House
Tulsa, Oklahoma

10 09 08 07 06   10 9 8 7 6 5 4 3 2 1

Dreams2Destiny Interactive Study Course:
Identify Your Gifts & Talents, Realize Your Life Calling,
Find True Fulfillment
ISBN 1-57794-780-0
Copyright © 2006 by Joseph S. Jones
8303-J East 111 St. South
Bixby, Oklahoma 74008

Published by Harrison House, Inc.
P.O. Box 35035
Tulsa, Oklahoma 74153

CONTENTS

Introduction

| Move further and go higher than you ever have before. | I remember as a little boy all the things I imagined I would grow up to be. My dream list was endless, but these were my top four picks: |

4. a fireman

3. an astronaut

2. a pro baseball player

1. one of the Beatles

My mom tells me I used to stand up like a rock star on my stage (the kitchen table), strum my guitar (my teddy bear), and sing the latest hits from the Fab Four. I'm sure it was quite a sight.

People say I had quite an imagination, but I believe I was just beginning to "dream dreams," as the Bible talks about.

And afterward, I will pour out my Spirit on all people. Your sons and daughters will prophesy, your old men will dream dreams, your young men will see visions.

Joel 2:28

God doesn't want to keep His plans a secret from you.

This prophecy from Joel was fulfilled on the Day of Pentecost, and the whole town of Jerusalem heard about it. When suddenly Christ's followers were unexplainably speaking in different languages, Peter stood up to address the baffled crowd:

"Men of Judea and all who dwell in Jerusalem, let this be known to you, and heed my words. For these are not drunk, as you suppose, since it is only the third hour of the day. But this is what was spoken by the prophet Joel: 'And it shall come to pass in the last days, says God, that I will pour out of My Spirit on all flesh; your sons and your daughters shall prophesy, your young men shall see visions, your old men shall dream dreams. And on My menservants and on My maidservants I will pour out My Spirit in those days; and they shall prophesy.'"

Acts 2:14-18

Through the Holy Spirit, God plants His dreams in human hearts even today. According to Jeremiah 29:11, those dreams are good ones:

I know the thoughts that I think toward you, says the Lord, thoughts of peace and not of evil, to give you a future and a hope.

God doesn't want to keep His plans a secret from you. He wants to prepare your heart with a vision and passion for those plans.

You've probably been around children full of anticipation for the wonderful future they envision for their lives. I believe this is the way God wants us all to be, and when we grow up He nudges us back to our dreams through the example of little children. But sadly, many times we fail to ignite kids' imaginations and, instead, help their flames of passion burn out.

In the church I pastor, The Landing Community Church, our mission has been to keep that imagination and passion alive in our kids. Our method is very simple: Find out what kids like to do, and throw God in the mix. Our youth group has a program called Tribal Arts, where the kids ("The Tribes") learn how to dance, film videos, write songs, and perform in dramas. Our desire is to fuel kids' imaginations and passion so that they can be all that God wants them to be.

He created you because of a dream, a vision, and a passion He carried inside just for you.

This book carries the same purpose for you. No matter your age or position in life, my desire is to fuel your imagination so that you see a bigger picture than the one you see now. Whether you're already on a successful career path or you're still looking for your niche, I want to enlighten your eyes to the vision of all that God has planned for you to be. I want to ignite your passion to move further and go higher than you ever have before.

As a child, you may have looked to things bigger and more exciting than what you were experiencing at the time, but those dreams may have fizzled away with time. If you want to explain those old dreams away, you could say they were just your way of escaping from reality. But maybe—just maybe—they were signs of your Maker instilling His wonderful creativity and vision in your heart and mind.

The Bible says that you are fearfully and wonderfully made.

For You formed my inward parts; You covered me in my mother's womb. I will praise You, for I am fearfully and wonderfully made; marvelous are Your works, and that my soul knows very well.

Psalm 139:13,14

God's works are wonderful, and you are His wonderful work. It shouldn't be too much for you to imagine that your Creator wants you to think out of the box and move toward a higher level of creativity—even now in your adulthood.

Perhaps you struggle with the whole idea of the Creator. Maybe you lean toward believing in Him, but haven't yet crossed the threshold between doubt and belief and begun a personal relationship with Him. As long as you have breath, it's never too late to seek Him. You can make that decision even now. Just ask the Lord to move into your life—to live in your heart—and choose to serve Him with all that is in you. You will be amazed as the emptiness you have always felt is filled by His love and purpose.

As you develop your relationship with the Creator, as you grow close to Him by reading His words in the Bible and praying, you will become increasingly creative. It only stands to reason that the closer you draw to someone, the more you will reflect that person's nature. Spending time with God will infinitely increase your creativity.

God is the first dreamer; He is the dream giver; and He is the dream fulfiller. He created you because of a dream, a vision, and a passion He carried inside just for you. The Bible says,

Your eyes saw my substance, being yet unformed. And in Your book they all were written, the days fashioned for me, when as yet there were none of them.

Psalm 139:16 NIV

Not only does God have a dream for you, but He implanted within you His ability to dream. When you pay attention to your dreams, you'll discover exactly who He intends you to be.

Your spiritual journey will begin with a vision of doing what God wants you to do (the dream), and will come to completion in His perfect will, where you are supernaturally effective for Him (your destiny). You've heard the word *destiny* all your life—in storybooks and maybe even in church—but most of us haven't given the word much thought. In this book, you'll be challenged not only to think about it, but to apply it to your own life.

> God orders not only your steps, but your stops as well. Don't let your divine rest stops become self-pity stops.

Destiny is something that is going to happen in the future. Notice I said it *is going to* happen. Your destiny is inevitable. It's certain. It's without a doubt. The word *destination* comes from the word *destiny.* Your destiny is your destination: It's where you are *certain* to end up.

The Bible says, "The steps of a good [or *righteous*] man are ordered by the Lord" (Psalm 37:23

NKJV). God is the director of your steps from dreams to destiny. To walk to the destiny He has for you, to be truly fulfilled, you need to know that He is interested in your success in every area of your life; that He has a plan for your physical, emotional, and spiritual health and prosperity. When you follow Him, you're taking His ordered steps toward the ultimate destiny He has planned for you.

God has a reward for you at the end of your spiritual journey. The Bible says, "...he who comes to God must believe that He is, and that He is a rewarder of those who diligently seek Him" (Hebrews 11:6). Notice the three steps in this verse. To come to God, you must (1) believe that He is, (2) believe that He is a rewarder, and (3) believe that He rewards those who diligently pursue Him.

As you diligently pursue God, He will direct your steps to destiny. Even so, that journey will not necessarily be an easy one. There will be seasons of laughter and seasons of tears. The Bible says there is a season for everything:

To everything there is a season, a time for every purpose under heaven.

Ecclesiastes 3:1

The important thing to remember is that, in every season, He will be with you. Through experience and observation, I've learned that God directs us on the dreams-to-destiny journey through five seasons of life: the dream, desperation, delay, divine assurance, and destiny. In the following pages, you will learn more about each of these seasons.

Along this journey, there will be times when you won't understand the process. At times, you may feel that you're doing more *stopping* than *stepping.* In those times, you must understand that God orders not only your steps, but your stops as well. Don't let your divine rest stops become self-pity stops.

God has your best interest at heart, and everything He does for and through you is for your benefit. God never said that life would be easy, but He did say that He would make you effective and walk through it with you. You can truly make a difference where you are right now. You can enlarge your influence by changing the way you perceive yourself and the way you perceive God.

When you grasp who you are in Christ as a child of your heavenly Father, it will be easy for you to understand that He wants the very best for you. You are a member of the royal family of God. Royal blood flows through your veins, and you are a joint-heir with Jesus. (Romans 8:17.) Imagine that! You are an heir to the inheritance of heaven! As a child of the rewarder and a joint-heir with Jesus, you have a future that looks ever brighter than your past and your present.

As you journey toward that bright future, take each season for what it is: a learning moment, a training session, growth and development time. Go through what you're going through, and let God make the way for you to achieve the dream He has planted within you.

Are you ready to escape the rut of just surviving?

Your journey to divine destiny is a unique process, and it will take you a different amount of time than it will take anyone else. They say overnight success takes ten years. No matter how long it seems to be taking, the key to reaching your destiny is keeping your hope along the way. You have to believe it can happen. "Without faith it is impossible to please God" (Hebrews 11:6). Keep the faith, no matter what.

Our scriptural basis for the journey through five seasons comes from Mark 5:22-43. It's the story of a synagogue ruler named Jairus and his journey from dreams to destiny. We will follow his journey in "A Father's Dream" through the five seasons in the pages ahead.

God has given each of us many dreams to direct us toward our ultimate destiny. As we follow Jairus's journey, I will share my personal story of walking through the five seasons of "The Stadium Dream" to fulfillment in destiny.

You, too, have been given dreams to fulfill in destiny, and that is what this book is all about. Following each chapter, you will have the opportunity to journal your progress through the seasons from dreams to destiny in "Evaluating Your Journey." Take an honest personal inventory along the way. You'll be amazed at all the things the Lord does for you if you will write about your journey and follow your spiritual progress.

Are you ready to dream again as you did when anything was possible? Are you ready to escape the rut of just surviving? You *can* do what God always intended you to do. I believe that when God looks for individuals to lead another step toward destiny, He looks for participants, not just observers. Observers aren't interested in playing. They never want the ball. Winners always want the ball. Are you ready to get off the couch, onto the court, down the lane, and to the net for that winning score?

Then turn the page, grab your Bible, journal your thoughts, renew your mind, think positively, and get ready to put legs on your faith. You're about to begin an adventure that will change your life forever: the journey from dreams to destiny!

SEASON 1

The Journey Begins With a Dream

Dreams are images of future possibilities.

On the journey to destiny, each of us begins with a dream. Whether you've discovered it or not, God has given you a vision and dream to be developed. The word *dream* is defined as "a strongly desired goal or purpose."[1] Dreams see details that will eventually come to pass.

Dreams are images of future possibilities. They see the impossible as possible, the unreachable as reachable, and the unattainable as attainable. A dream sees hoped-for, future events as present fact.

As a child, I was one of the Beatles! It was already fact to me.

Your dream may be to start a flourishing business, compete in a triathlon, work in ministry, or successfully raise a child. Whatever your

Dreams require you to get outside of yourself so you can see within yourself.

dream, it will blend in with your spiritual calling and the ultimate destiny God has planned for you.

Many times God will use dreams to ignite and inspire us, to provide us with hope for our future. Other times, He will use dreams to help us avoid trouble ahead and to direct us around and over the obstacles on the path to our destiny.

The path starts with a dream. If you haven't identified your dream, ask God today to help you begin to dream His dreams for you. You can dream big or small—but if you're going to be dreaming anyway, you may as well dream big!

Someone once asked me if I dreamed in 5x7 or 8x10. They were asking whether I dream small or enlarge the picture. In my lifetime, God has given me many dreams and walked with me many times to fulfillment in destiny. I know that each dream and its fulfillment is another step toward my ultimate destiny, and I have learned that God doesn't give me dreams that He can't help me fulfill. So I don't dream in 5x7 anymore; my dreams are so big—they're like billboards!

Dreams take the limits off of you and off of God. Dreams require you to get outside of yourself so you can see within yourself and allow God to shape you into the person He created you to be. Faith has a way of working with your dreams so that you see yourself doing things you can't do on your own, accomplishing the vision with God by your side.

It's only impossible until somebody does it—and that somebody may as well be you! Once you lock into your calling and begin to see yourself doing the impossible for God, He will make it possible for you. When He plants a dream in your heart, He will walk beside you through every season until you reach your destiny. That is exactly what He did for a man named Jairus.

THE BIRTH OF
A FATHER'S DREAM

Now when Jesus had crossed over again by boat to the other side, a great multitude gathered to Him; and He was by the sea. And behold, one of the rulers of the synagogue came, Jairus by name.

Mark 5:21-24 (NKJV)

I like to believe that Jairus could be compared to any good, churchgoing, community-serving, loving husband and father that we know. My instincts tell me that he was faithful in the little things and was blessed in life as a result, because Jesus said:

3

Whoever can be trusted with very little can also be trusted with much....

Luke 16:10 NIV

The Bible also says that a married man finds favor with God and that children are a reward from the Lord. (Proverbs 18:22, Psalm 127:3.) Jairus was not only a devoted husband and father, but was a faithful leader in God's house as a synagogue ruler. This man wasn't a pew potato; he mixed it up for God and actively participated in His work.

In the Bible account, we learn that Jairus is the father of a twelve-year-old daughter. We aren't made aware of her name, but it would be safe to assume that she was his pride and joy. That if Kodak would've had a one-hour photo store in Jerusalem, he would've carried around her picture as her proud dad. That when she was a newborn, he rocked her in his arms and sang sweet Hebrew lullabies until she fell asleep. And that as she slept, he watched her and envisioned her growing into a beautiful woman, a loving bride, and a wonderful mother.

As a godly father, Jairus gave his life, his time, and his energy to ensuring that his child's goals and aspirations would not only be probable but possible. He desired the very best for her and wanted to see her grow up to be all that she could be for God.

As the father of three beautiful children, I know what that feels like. My wife and I would do anything for our kids! We might have times when we pretend they belong to someone else (like in the restaurant when our daughter tosses her roll onto the table next to ours!), but we do strive to set a good example for them and raise them with the proper tools to be successful. The Bible says that when we train our children in the way they should go, they will not stray away from that godly instruction when they grow older.

Train up a child in the way he should go, and when he is old he will not depart from it.

Proverbs 22:6

That is my dream, and I know it was Jairus's dream too.

Jairus had plans for his little girl. Surely he and his mother had carefully prepared their newborn daughter's first dress to wear to the synagogue. Holding their precious girl, Jairus must have envisioned her happy wedding day; and every day he must have vigilantly protected her from anyone or anything that would interfere with that dream. Someday he knew he would walk his princess down the aisle and place her little hand into the hand of the one man who would be able to care for the beautiful bride as she deserved.

It's easy to imagine the emotion Jairus felt visualizing this dream and the energy he spent ensuring its success. At the beginning of his journey from dream to destiny, he never could have imagined what despair lay ahead.

THE BEGINNING OF
THE STADIUM DREAM

Without a doubt, my most memorable journey from dream to destiny came in the fall of 1994 while I was producing the *Raising the Standard* tour with Carman. This was an incredible tour, featuring songs like "Who's in the House?" "Great God," and "America Again." During this tour, we collected more than 1 million signatures on a petition to bring prayer back into the United States public school systems. It was a year when everything held great meaning and purpose for me. Life was good, and I felt God more than ever in everything that I did.

As we prepared for the tour, I sensed that Carman was feeling something in his heart. After spending nearly twenty years in ministry with him, I knew that without hearing him say it. But I didn't yet know what God was preparing him for.

In all of our tours past, we'd held our concerts in just about every arena and auditorium you could mention. Those concerts were great, but Carman wanted more—and I did too.

We'd signed a record deal with Liberty Records and met one of the most influential icons in the business, Jimmy Bowen, who became a tremendous friend of the ministry. It's easy to respect someone who does a great job, and Bowen was great at what he did. He knew the business. He knew how to get results and sell records—and we knew how to produce live events. Without a doubt, this would be an incredible partnership. It was the biggest record deal Carman had ever signed, and it would be the catalyst for his biggest concert event.

About the time Carman was feeling restless about venues and shows, we received an invitation to a concert of another Liberty recording artist—country western singer Garth Brooks—at Texas Stadium. Little did we know it, but God was preparing to show us something exciting about faith.

Carman and I headed to Dallas to see just what a stadium concert with the world's top country western artist looked like. It was quite a production. Lights were everywhere, and the crowd was very much into all the showmanship. Everything was flying through the air: beer, peanuts—even Garth!

As we sat in what felt like a 70,000-seat honky-tonk, hearing the crowd sing about their friends in low places, the Lord began planting a dream in our hearts. I remember Carman getting up from his seat and saying he would be back in a moment. While he was gone, I continued to study all of the elements of this huge production—everything from the stage to the costumes and lights. I was looking at what it would take to do something like this. After what seemed nearly an hour, Carman came back. Later I found out that he'd been walking around the stadium, like Joshua around the city of Jericho, ready to take it for God. (See Joshua 5-6.) He looked at me as if to say, "Brace yourself: I've just seen God, and here is what He said!"

Somehow I knew what he was going to say. He'd said it so many times before about seemingly impossible things: "I think we need to do this for the Lord," he said with a smile.

I smiled, and my mind immediately started the categorical exercise of planning a stadium concert.

EVALUATING YOUR JOURNEY

Season 1: The Dream

Is your life fulfilling right now?

Are you completely happy?

Are you doing what you always knew you would do?

Most of us couldn't answer these questions with a resounding *yes*.

God has given each of us a reason for being—a purpose for living. That purpose will be accomplished, and your sense of fulfillment will come, as you move in the direction of the dream inside.

A dream is all that you need to start the journey to your destiny. Once God puts the dream in you, it will take over—if you let it. I remember once hearing T. D. Jakes say, "God didn't give you a dream for you to do it. He gave you a dream for you to watch it."

As you evaluate your journey, you will begin to identify your God-given dream. When you discover it and start pursuing activities surrounding it, you'll begin to see a complete shift in your moods, your attitude, and your personal success. Get out your Bible and your pen, and prepare to discover fulfillment, happiness, and purpose as you discover your God-given dreams.

One way to discover your dreams is to realize what makes you happy. What are some activities that you enjoy doing? What makes you happy?

_____

_____

_____

_____

_____

_____

_____

_____

_____

_____

_____

_____

Another exercise that can help you pinpoint your dream is to consider what you would do with your life "in a perfect world." If you had all the resources you needed and could do anything at all, what would you choose to do?

_____

_____

_____

_____

_____

_____

_____

_____

_____

_____

_____

_____

_____

Dreams are images of future possibilities. Do you have a dream that you believe the Lord has planted in your spirit? What does it look like? What do you see yourself doing with God's help?

_____

_____

_____

_____

_____

_____

_____

_____

_____

_____

_____

_____

_____

What Scriptures support your dreams?

_____

_____

_____

_____

_____

_____

_____

_____

_____

_____

_____

_____

_____

_____

_____

_____

_____

You need a target if you want to start shooting. How will your dream become your destiny? List five short-term goals that you would like to begin accomplishing immediately.

_____

_____

_____

_____

_____

_____

_____

_____

_____

_____

_____

_____

List five long-term goals that you would like to accomplish this year or in the more distant future.

_____

_____

_____

_____

_____

_____

_____

_____

_____

_____

_____

_____

_____

_____

Journal your thoughts about your dreams.

_____

_____

_____

_____

_____

_____

_____

_____

_____

_____

_____

_____

_____

_____

_____

_____

SEASON 2

Disrupted by Desperation

Despair is the enemy's way of taking our eyes off the dream.

It feels great when God initiates a dream in your spirit and you sense a fire burning deep within you to walk toward your destiny, but the journey isn't always filled with that overwhelming sense of excitement and assurance. When you launch out into a work for the kingdom of God, adversity will inevitably lunge toward you. There will always be a cost that comes with following your God-given dream.

Many years ago my wife and I took a trip to Kansas City. At the time, we were living in Tulsa and had only one child, our infant son Brandon. We were just learning how to deal with the responsibility of parenthood, but feeling we had a pretty good handle on this "raising a child" thing, we were ready for a weekend journey together as a family. We packed the car, or I should say Bridgette packed the car—with everything but the crib! She was convinced there would be nothing at the hotel for the baby to do, so we just *had* to take the entire toy chest with us!

Meanwhile, being a planner, I mapped out the route we would travel, how long it would take us to get there, and where we would stop for fuel and breaks for sanity's sake. I was meticulous, and I must say the planning was exquisite. Every detail was covered. The hotel was booked and confirmed, the car was packed, and finally we launched out on our getaway.

We made great time, and before we knew it signs were indicating that we were coming into Kansas City. I was getting very excited because there was a great gadget store there and I love gadgets. The entire trip was going so well!

But suddenly it happened.

The door to hell came off the hinges as the onslaught began. The demons of confusion and disruption had been unleashed and told to bring Joe Jones much torment.

Unbelievably, my directions to the hotel were wrong, and I couldn't find it! Like any good man, I drove around for more than half an hour without asking for directions. My forehead was drenched in perspiration, and anger was beginning to swell inside me. I had not planned for this! How could this have happened?

After countless trips around several blocks, seemingly going in circles, I somehow ended up in the parking lot of our hotel. I had conquered—without asking for directions!

With somewhat of an arrogant, prideful smile on my face, I jumped out of the car and went into the office to register. When I received my room assignment, I realized it had to be at the top of the hotel, on a floor in the double digits. While normally that wouldn't be a problem, I was about to learn a lesson in parenting: Never stay anywhere but on the first floor when you have a small child and your wife packs *all* the toys!

I must have made twenty trips back and forth bringing in all of the various baby necessities. Finally, all items had been delivered and we were all moved in. I looked at Bridgette, she looked at me, and we smiled at each other. We had arrived, unpacked, and were about to do something we both love to do: Shop!

We hadn't been in our room more than half an hour before we were off to the mall to see what we could find. First, I would be rewarded with a stop at the gadget store. You see, I am a collector of gadgets: briefcases, day timers, and such, and this store had so much for me to experience! I'm what they call an "early adopter," which simply means that I pay the highest possible retail price for any new, cool gadget because I *have* to have it first.

So when we got to this store, I had officially arrived! It was total bliss! I'd already forgotten about the trauma of finding the hotel, and somehow my back was no longer hurting from the luggage workout I'd endured. Now we were happy, loving life, and enjoying all that this world had to offer.

However, the demons of torment were still hovering. Brandon must have gotten dizzy from all of the shopping—wheeling in and out of every store. The mall was closing, and we were heading back to the hotel when it happened.

On the journey from dreams to destiny, the strongest feelings of disappoint- ment come when the journey doesn't go as planned and it seems the dream is gone.

Brandon became violently sick. In fact, every couple of minutes he was throwing up all over the car. Another thing I had not planned for! I had not factored in projectile vomiting on this trip. I was totally unprepared for this.

Bridgette was the calm one, somewhat scared but still a pillar of strength. I was a total basket case—one hand on the wheel, one hand blocking this little heaving machine and wiping up a substance I'd never seen before. I was driving around in circles, praying, yelling, questioning—you name it, I was doing it.

It was getting close to midnight, and now because I'd been driving around in circles, I was lost again. I didn't know how to return to the hotel. I hadn't asked for directions to the hotel during the day, so you can surely guess what I did at midnight in this strange town: I kept driving and driving—until frustration met exhaustion, and my fear for my son purged out my inner pride.

My wife and I decided Brandon needed a certain drink that we'd heard would help keep him from becoming dehydrated. Miraculously we happened upon a twenty-four-hour supermarket, and I walked in while Bridgette and Brandon waited in the car.

I must confess, now, I was so frazzled by the recent chain of events that I was somewhat out of my mind.

As I walked into the store, I began to see and feel a strange spirit gripping me: Fear! You should've seen the type of people in that store after midnight on a weekend! I ran wildly to the baby section, grabbed the drink, checked out, and ran back to the car. By this time, my eyes were looking at each other, and I'm sure my wife wondered who in the world she'd married. I must have looked like Marty Feldman on caffeine!

We finally made it back to the hotel. After an hour or two, though, Brandon was not doing much better—so we decided to return home.

The journey hadn't gone at all according to my plan, and all of the difficulty had stolen my joy and flooded my heart with disappointment.

On the journey from dreams to destiny, the strongest feelings of disappointment come when the journey doesn't go as planned and it seems the dream is gone. It's in this season of desperation that many people lose the passion to continue the journey.

Jairus, of all people, knew this to be true.

DESPAIR DISRUPTS
A FATHER'S DREAM

I can only imagine the disappointment Jairus experienced when his beautiful daughter fell ill. Ever since his wife had announced her pregnancy with the child, Jairus had carried a dream for his little girl, a journey mapped out in his mind. But somehow along the way, something had gone terribly wrong. Suddenly the apple of his eye was lying in bed at the door of death. This was not part of the dream. This was nowhere in the vision of his daughter, son-in-law, and little grandchildren coming home for holidays. This was not in the plan!

There weren't supposed to be any problems a father couldn't handle, but something was wrong with his little girl, and he couldn't fix it. Despair firmly grasped Jairus's heart, and all he could do was pace back and forth, trying to figure out how to make everything all right.

Despair is the enemy's way of taking our eyes off the dream. Despair cripples the mind and paralyzes the spirit until we become incapacitated. We can't think straight, we act irrational, and our planning and attention to detail dissipate. The journey comes to a complete stop.

Many people abandon their dreams and walk away from their destiny, but you can make it if you realize that disappointments are an unavoidable part of the journey toward destiny. Anytime you attempt to give your time, talent, finances, and energy toward a godly cause, you can expect opposition. The devil doesn't like spiritual progress, so if you're moving forward on your path from dreams to destiny, start watching for the attack. Prepare yourself for it.

The first place the enemy will attack is your mind. His goal is to change the way you think about yourself. He'll tell you you're powerless in the face of adversity. He'll nag at you with the fear that in time you will lose everything. He'll taunt you, saying, "This is what you get for serving the Lord."

When he does, just remember that the devil is a liar! His only plan is to sow seeds of fear into your mind because fear is the exact opposite of faith. Fear believes that the absolute worst will happen, but faith believes that the absolute best will happen. God didn't give you a spirit of fear but rather of power, love, and a sound mind. (1 Timothy 1:7.) A sound mind is one that knows how to distinguish between right and

Feelings of despair always seem to surface on the eve of the miraculous.

wrong; a mind that is able to choose God's way over the devil's way.

In order to conquer fear and the devil's attacks on your mind, you have to know what the Bible says you can do. James 4:7 says:

Submit yourselves, then, to God. Resist the devil, and he will flee from you.

At this point in the journey, you can't afford to be timid. You're on your way to destiny, and no devil in hell has the power to keep you from getting there! Greater is the God who is in you than the devil that is after you.

You are of God, little children, and have overcome them, because He who is in you is greater than he who is in the world.

1 John 4:4

You say, "Joe, that sounds great, but Jairus was about to lose his little girl!"

Or "I had a dream, but the pressure was just too much."

Or "How can you be so positive when the situation seems terminal?"

My answer is simple. I believe that nothing good ever comes of being negative. There is no benefit in doubt.

Doubt disengages, but faith engages. Positive thinking produces positive results, and I choose to believe that the absolute best can happen in any situation in life.

Doubt is like a rocking chair. You can do it all day, but you're not getting anywhere. But faith in God can take you to places you've only dreamed about. With God, all things are possible! (Matthew 19:26.) In an instant, everything can change for the good. And, according to Romans 8:28, all things are working together for your benefit:

And we know that all things work together for good to those who love God, to those who are the called according to His purpose.

God will work everything together for your good when you trust Him and love Him.

Without fail, the greatest victories and celebrations come through trials and disappointments. When you hit this season of disappointment, the only way to keep your passion is to stay focused on the end of the journey—your destiny.

Feelings of despair always seem to surface on the eve of the miraculous.

If you want something you've never had, you have to do something you've never done.

Jairus could attest to that.

When he heard that Jesus was on His way across the lake, his spirit surely leaped inside him. He'd heard all about the miraculous events that followed the carpenter's son, and now this famous Healer had stepped on his shore.

Jairus was desperate, and desperate times call for desperate measures. When his dream for his little girl began to crumble, he searched for Jesus and literally fell at His feet when he found Him.

And when he saw Him, he fell at His feet and begged Him earnestly, saying, "My little daughter lies at the point of death."

Mark 5:22,23

Jairus wasn't concerned about what it looked like for a refined, dignified ruler of the synagogue to be kneeling in the mud in front of this controversial prophet. He tossed aside the status quo, public opinion, and political bureaucracy, and pled for his dream to stay alive.

When you really want something, you go after it with all that's in you. If you want something you've never had, you have to do something you've never done.

Many times people jump with both feet into a personal fantasy, only to find themselves in over their heads and sinking fast. They may have interpreted their fantasy as a dream from God, but in reality it was just last night's burrito and salsa. When despair comes, they find themselves further from God than ever before.

However, when God puts the dream inside of you, despair will only draw you closer to Him.

Don't let despair take your eyes off your destiny. Hebrews 12:1-2 says:

> *...let us run with endurance the race that is set before us,*
> *looking unto Jesus, the author and finisher of our faith,*
> *who for the joy that was set before Him endured the*
> *cross, despising the shame, and has sat down at the right*
> *hand of the throne of God.*

Fix your eyes on Jesus, the author and the finisher of your faith. He will be there at the beginning of your journey to see that you get out of the starting blocks, and you can be sure that if you endure the race, He'll be there at the finish line. As you reach the destination He set before you, He'll stand waiting for you with a big smile on His face.

He's never early, and He's never late. He's always right on time with the answer!

When desperation hits, keep your eyes on Jesus. He'll make sure you get to your destination, when you focus on Him.

Keeping the dream alive and finishing the race require determination and focus. Don't focus on the desperation, or you'll lose your destination. Keep your eyes on the prize!

Perhaps you're a singer and you know God wants you to sing for Him, but maybe you haven't been able to break out of your own hometown and your dream seems somewhat neglected. Whether you dream of singing or selling, ministering or managing, if you're feeling stuck in your journey from dreams to destiny, then you need to know one tried-and-true principle: When you deepen your ministry, God will broaden it.

In other words, you need to keep applying what you know in the position where you serve God now, and you need to trust Him for the promotional plan. You will be promoted when you become overqualified where you are.

But it won't be a breeze.

Are you ready to pay the price that comes with pursuing your dream? If you aren't willing to go through the fire, as our friends Shadrach, Meshach, and Abednego were, then don't expect to come out of the fire untouched. (See Daniel 3.) The devil is a dream thief who wants not only to destroy your dream, but to destroy you. Get ready for disappointment and discouragement. No, they're not comfortable, but they will force you to keep running back into the arms of the Dream Giver, who will keep you on the path to destiny.

When a situation seems hopeless, you'll have to rely on your only hope: Jesus Christ. Friends will let you down. Family members will not come through for you all the time. People will let you down, so you'll have to find a way to put your faith in God. Remember: He's never early, and He's never late. He's always right on time with the answer!

"But what about those voices that keep discouraging me?" you ask.

Remember that the devil wants to infiltrate your mind with thoughts that you can't accomplish your God-given destiny. Second Corinthians 10:5 tells us what to do in response to his discouragement:

Casting down arguments and every high thing that exalts itself against the knowledge of God, bringing every thought into captivity to the obedience of Christ.

Only through the Spirit of God can you find the weapons needed to demolish those discouraging thoughts. *The Message* Bible version says, "We use our powerful God-tools for smashing warped philosophies, tearing down barriers erected against the truth of God...." With the tools provided by the Spirit of God, "we are destroying specula-tions..." (NAS) and "We demolish arguments..." (NIV).

We destroy speculations and demolish arguments and every discouraging thought that enters our minds with the spiritual tools God has given us. Praying and speaking the Scriptures are two of those tools that will pull down strongholds, cast down arguments, and bring our thoughts into subjection to Christ. (vv. 4,5.)

If a thought isn't constructive, then it's destructive. If it doesn't edify, encourage, and build up your spiritual walk, then it's not from God. And if a thought is not of God, then you need to use your "God-tools" to demolish it.

Next time you have a thought that you know hasn't been sent by God, just say, "God has given me authority to take that thought captive and resist it from entering my mind and my spirit." Remember: 2 Corinthians 10:4-5 says, "For the weapons of our warfare are...mighty in God for pulling down strongholds...bringing every thought into captivity to the obedience of Christ." No destructive thought can stand against the authority God has given you.

Sometimes, even when you know God is there with you in the battle, you can still feel all alone. This is when you need to seek out support from the body of Christ. You need to be accountable to your local pastor and to other Christians. If you're facing discouragement, then find a prayer partner—a friend you can confide in who will agree with you and believe with you as you walk your journey of faith. Learn from the testimonies of others, and let their victories encourage you. God is no respecter of persons: What He does for your neighbor, He can and will do for you.

Make up your mind today to not give way to thoughts of desperation, and keep your eyes focused on where you're going.

Stay busy. If you abandon activity and become stagnant, you'll soon begin to feel sorry for yourself and lose the momentum and desire to move forward.

It may take some sacrifice. It will take a great deal of determination, but remember: If you want something you've never had, you'll have to do something you've never done. Prepare yourself for it.

DESPERATION HITS
THE STADIUM DREAM

After Carman and I flew back to Nashville, I found myself consumed by the idea of producing a stadium event. Texas Stadium was an incredible facility, and we would be the first contemporary Christian solo act to try something this huge. That gave me the push I needed. I liked pioneering new highways.

It truly appeared that this dream would become reality—until, one day, desperation hit.

I set up an appointment to fly to Dallas and meet the stadium's general manager to see just what it would take to do an event like this.

It was an interesting first meeting. The general manager showed me the autographed guitar on his wall that Garth had presented to him as a thank-you for his events there. I felt like he thought this was a bit too much for us.

Part of me was nervous, and part was in awe of the potential of this dream. I imagine it was like being at the edge of an incredible waterfall: seeing its beauty, hearing its roar, and knowing that you are going over the edge any second!

I was filled with a faith I had never felt before. I felt like David in King Saul's presence, saying, "Let me at the Philistine giant, for I can surely take him." (See 1 Samuel 17.) I really believed in the possibility of this dream, and I wanted very much to do this.

I showed the general manager videos of events we had done in a large stadium in South Africa, to which even Nelson Mandela had come. I showed him the altar calls and young and old alike accepting Christ into their hearts as Carman preached and sang.

As the general manager witnessed the awesome power of Christ at work in these events, our conversation changed. The feeling we had about the possibility for a Christ-centered concert of this magnitude changed, too. Over the next few months, many meetings would take place to review facility layouts, procedures, logistics, and expenses.

We were going to do this concert on a "love offering" basis. All of Carman Ministries' events were done this way. We would always rely on God to bring it all together and cover the costs.

All of our planning for this event was running so smoothly, and it truly appeared that this dream would become reality—until, one day, desperation hit.

After many meetings, the general manager informed me that the Dallas Cowboys would get the first shot at dates. They had to finalize their schedule before we could be guaranteed a date, and that would not happen until July. Here we were in the first quarter of the year, gearing up for this event, putting things in place, and talking it up with everyone. *I couldn't wait till July to promote an October event of this size!* That just wouldn't be enough time!

What was I going to do? How could all of this enthusiasm be snuffed out at this point? It all looked so good! This was Carman's dream—and mine too!

Just as Jairus fell on his knees before Jesus on the shore that day and pleaded for the life of his little girl, I was pleading with God for the life of this dream. I implored Him to point me to the right date. But I wasn't on a lakeshore. I was 30,000 feet in the air, heading back to Tulsa to tell the staff the unfortunate news.

As I reviewed the possible dates on the schedule, my frustration kept rising. I was trying to route many cities in the fall; Dallas was only one of them. The Texas Stadium concert had to be on a Saturday, and we had to have setup time. None of the open dates fit into our tour schedule—except one.

EVALUATING YOUR JOURNEY

Season 2: Desperation

Has the enemy planted seeds of fear on your path? Most people abandon their dreams at the first sign of adversity because they're paralyzed by fear. Fear that is mismanaged and ignored will eventually turn into despair.

Every person who has begun a new thing—a new job, business, or relationship—has faced despair. Despair is simply the feeling that what you've set out to do won't happen. The danger of despair is that it can take your mind off of the dream you've just discovered and become your great obstacle to progress on your journey to destiny.

The first two steps toward solving any problem are (1) recognizing that something is wrong and (2) desiring to fix it. *Faith is the antidote to fear. So if you desire to fix the fear problem,* just believe that the absolute best will happen and you'll keep running in the right direction.

What is your greatest fear?

_____

_____

What do you usually do when you're afraid?

_____

_____

_____

_____

_____

_____

_____

_____

_____

_____

_____

_____

_____

_____

_____

How do you feel about the unknown? Does it intrigue you or frighten you?

_____

_____

_____

_____

_____

_____

_____

_____

_____

_____

_____

_____

_____

_____

_____

_____

If you were to remove fear from your life, how would you be different?
What could you do if you had no fear?

_____

_____

_____

_____

_____

_____

_____

_____

_____

_____

_____

_____

_____

What types of situations have caused you to despair in the past?

_____

_____

_____

_____

_____

_____

_____

_____

_____

_____

_____

_____

_____

_____

_____

The antidote to despair is faith. Faith believes that the best can and will happen. What good things might come out of you if you were to become consistently positive?

_____

_____

_____

_____

_____

_____

_____

_____

_____

_____

_____

_____

What Scriptures can help you overcome fear and, therefore, despair on your journey from dreams to destiny?

_____

_____

_____

_____

_____

_____

_____

_____

_____

_____

_____

_____

_____

_____

One sure thing in life is that people will try to bring despair when you pursue your dreams. They will say, "It can't happen," or "You're wasting your time." At the very least, they'll make sure you know your dream is a long shot. What will you do when people try to bring you discouragement?

_____

_____

_____

_____

_____

_____

_____

_____

_____

_____

_____

_____

_____

Who are some people you can turn to for encouragement and account-
ability when you feel yourself dipping into despair?

_____

_____

_____

_____

_____

_____

_____

_____

_____

_____

_____

_____

_____

_____

Hebrews 12:2 tells us to keep "looking unto Jesus, the author and finisher of our faith...." How will you keep your focus on Jesus instead of despair?

_____

_____

_____

_____

_____

_____

_____

_____

_____

_____

_____

_____

_____

If you do find yourself in despair, don't stay there. Keep your mind sharp and your eyes on the prize! (1 Corinthians 9:24.) Imagine and describe the day you will reach your destiny and obtain your prize.

Journal your thoughts about desperation.

_____

_____

_____

_____

_____

_____

_____

_____

_____

_____

_____

_____

_____

_____

_____

_____

_____

_____

DREAMS 2 DESTINY

SEASON 3

Warning: Delays Ahead

Delays are God's waiting room.

As I was traveling down the interstate, I noticed a flashing yellow sign urging me to take another road to avoid heavy traffic: "Detour Ahead."

As usual, my first reaction to that detour sign was panic. *Where will the detour take me?* I wondered. *How far out of the way will I go, and how long will it take to return to the original course?*

Detours and delays always seem to go hand in hand. Let's face it: Nobody enjoys delays. I have yet to hear anyone say, "Oh, I wish I could've sat a bit longer in that traffic on the interstate!" or "Why did they bring me my food so quickly? I would like to just sit here and enjoy the restaurant!" No, most of us get all bent out of shape at the very sound of the word *delay.* We always hope to find the word *short* in front of it!

Detours and delays most often come when we need to be some-where in a hurry or when we're late for an important appointment. Jairus knew exactly what that felt like.

DELAY DISRUPTS
A FATHER'S DREAM

Jairus had said to Jesus, essentially, "If You'll just come to the house and lay Your hands on my daughter, I know she'll be all right." (v. 23.) Faith moves God. Jesus saw the faith of this father and began to walk toward the house, as if to say, "Okay, let's go do it!"

By this time, we know that hope had been injected into Jairus's soul. When Jairus had desperately asked for Jesus' help, he knew they would need to get to his daughter as quickly as possible. Getting home was the only thing on his mind. The One with supernatural power was on the way to keep his dream alive. In fact, many others were touched by this display of compassion, and the Bible says that the multitudes moved with them.

Imagine what Jairus felt during that walk. *This feels good!* he must have thought. *We're on our way! Soon the drama will be over, and she'll be healed!* Not only had he been able to ask the Healer to come, but now they were walking side by side on their way to take care of business!

The stress must have lifted off of Jairus as he looked at Jesus. He must have noticed that Jesus didn't appear shaken at all. There was no sign of worry on His face, no visible evidence of any internal doubt. It was as if He already knew the outcome of this trip.

The sun began to shine through the gray clouds. The situation was changing, and a brighter day lay ahead. But then, suddenly, delay came.

Now a certain woman had a flow of blood for twelve years, and had suffered many things from many physicians. She had spent all that she had and was no better, but rather grew worse. When she heard about Jesus, she came behind Him in the crowd and touched His garment. For she said, "If only I may touch His clothes, I shall be made well."

Mark 5:25-28

Jairus noticed that suddenly they weren't walking anymore. They were standing still, and Jesus looked puzzled. "Who touched Me?" He asked over the noise of the multitude of people asking why they were stopping here.

Immediately the fountain of her blood was dried up, and she felt in her body that she was healed of the affliction. And Jesus, immediately knowing in Himself that power had gone out of Him, turned around in the crowd and said, "Who touched My clothes?"

I like to think of delays as God's waiting room.
Nobody likes to sit in the waiting room, but we do it.

But His disciples said to Him, "You see the multitude thronging You, and You say, 'Who touched Me?'"

Mark 5:29-31

Then the disciples started to speak, "What do You mean, who touched You? Can't You see this crowd pressing in against You?"

Yet Jesus persisted. He'd felt healing power leave His body. "Who touched Me?" He turned, looking all around Him, until He was facing the lake they had just come from.

And He looked around to see her who had done this thing.

Mark 5:32

Now suddenly, the crowd became aware of a woman sprawled out on the ground, her hand holding the edge of Jesus' garment. Some of them even began to recognize her.

But the woman, fearing and trembling, knowing what had happened to her, came and fell down before Him and told Him the whole truth.

Mark 5:33

For twelve years she had been ill, visiting doctors' offices frequently, and had spent all of her money trying to beat this illness that had held her in its grip. Everyone was waiting with hopeful anticipation to see what would happen to this woman.

Everyone, that is, except Jairus.

By this point, Jairus must have become unsettled, perhaps even angry. He was desperate! He had fallen on his knees *in the mud* to beg Jesus to heal his little girl. Had that meant *nothing* to Jesus? They had begun the journey toward his house, but this woman had messed everything up and grabbed hold of his only hope! This woman had captured Jesus' attention and turned Him around—away from Jairus's dying daughter!

Can't you just imagine Jairus's thoughts? *Look, Jesus: That lady has been sick for twelve years! Another day isn't going to hurt her! Why are You stopping? She can make it another day! You can tend to her on the way back! My daughter will die if we don't hurry! Don't You care about that anymore?*

Suddenly, Jairus's eyes were no longer on the Healer, but on the one who needed healing.

Is this where we are today? Are we so consumed by our need that we have no time for delays? Are we missing the miracles in our midst

Delays are simply circum- stances that we must walk through to build our faith and refine our walk with Him.

by looking at the delay and not the divine? I think all of us face delay, as Jairus must have that day, with disappointment.

While a stranger among the crowd was receiving a long-awaited miracle, he was thinking about his own situation and wondering why Jesus had forgotten about him.

Many of us have been in this position, wondering, "Why have You forgotten about my needs, Lord? Don't You care about me anymore?"

In those moments, we have to remember that delays are not God's denials. Delays aren't even always bad.

In our rushed lives, we tend to look at delays or detours as inter- ruptions, as events that occur at an inopportune time. However, many times a delay turns out to be the best thing that could have happened. It may provide some time for things to work out better for a business deal, for example, or it may make a friendship stronger. Many times, delays become the defining moments in our lives.

I like to think of delays as God's waiting room. Nobody likes to sit in the waiting room, but we do it. We wait because we have a hope that we'll see the physician and get a prescription for medicine that will cure what ails us. In God's waiting room, we can wait with the hope that the Physician will bind our wounds and cure what ails us so that we can successfully journey to our destiny. Changing the way we view waiting is mandatory for those who will make it through the five seasons from dreams to destiny.

So the next time you experience a delay on your journey, don't immediately assume it's bad. See it in a positive light. Maybe the Lord is holding you back from a major pit that would swallow you up if you kept moving ahead. Maybe He wants you to learn how to heal someone else along the way to your healing. In the Bible, God tells us to pray one for another that we may be healed. (James 5:16.)

Most of all, just remember: Delays are not denials; the answer is on the way!

The devil knows this, too, so when we face delay he always tries to convince us that God has abandoned us mid-journey. He says, "No one could love you. God certainly doesn't. You're not worthy enough to be called a Christian. That's why you haven't gotten your prayers answered." Remember that the devil is the sower of discord among God's people. (Proverbs 6:14.) He is the author of confusion. (1 Corinthians 14:33.) The Bible says that where there is envy and confusion, there are all other types of evil at work too. (James 3:16.)

We need to learn how to let these periods of waiting work for us, not against us. The Bible tells us to "let patience have its perfect work, that you may be perfect and complete, lacking nothing" (James 1:4).

Delays are simply circumstances that we must walk through to build our faith and refine our walk with Him. If we will have patience in God's waiting room, He will develop our character so that we can move to the next step toward our destiny.

God commits to character, not talent. According to 2 Timothy 2:2, He works with people who are reliable and qualified. Ability may get you a shot at the top and may even take you there, but your character will keep you there.

Remember that 1 Corinthians 9:24 says to run in such a way as to win the prize. On your journey from dreams to destiny, you are aiming for victory. You don't live a life of mediocrity, because you know that God wants the absolute best for you in every way. He wants to bless you exceedingly and abundantly above all that you could ever imagine. (Ephesians 3:20.) In order to prepare you for the blessing, He works on your character. He helps you grow inside in areas like trustworthiness, respect, responsibility, fairness, caring, and citizenship. He helps you become qualified for the prize you're heading for.

If you are sensing a delay, look around you and watch for a miracle.

Helen Keller said, "Character cannot be developed in ease and quiet. Only through the experience of trial and suffering can the soul be strengthened, vision cleared, ambition inspired, and success achieved."[2] Such growing pains most often occur in the middle of delay, but their purpose is to strengthen you for the end of your journey when you cross the finish line and obtain the prize.

Please realize that it may not be easy, but as you press on God will make you effective and walk through it with you. You can truly make a difference where you are right now. Even in the middle of delay, you can enlarge your influence by changing the way you perceive yourself and the way you perceive Him.

You see, your need is significant to the Lord and His desire is to see you made whole; to see you overcome every obstacle and win the victory in your life. Don't give up hope. He is always at work. If you are sensing a delay, look around you and watch for a miracle.

Jesus was on the way to do a miracle for Jairus, but someone else needed healed on the way. This woman, like Jairus, was also desperate, and she believed that all she had to do was touch Jesus and she would be well again. She heard about Him, she sought Him out, and she pressed in to get what she knew He had to give her. And her persistence paid off.

Romans 2:5-7 NIV says,

God "will give to each person according to what he has done." To those who by persistence in doing good seek glory, honor and immortality, he will give eternal life.

In the *New King James* version of this verse, persistence is called "patient continuance." This is what this woman had, and she received her miracle. And this is what you must have in order to successfully journey from dreams to destiny.

To develop persistence, or patient continuance, in your life, you will need to master the art of prayer: communication with your Creator.

In Matthew 7:7, Jesus told us about three types of prayer.

"Ask, and it will be given to you; seek, and you will find; knock, and it will be opened to you."

Ask. Seek. Knock. These three words identify three different actions that will take you to three different levels of success on your journey to your divine destiny.

Many times I've heard people say to persistent people, "Why do you have to keep praying for the same thing? Don't you think God heard you the first time?" Then I read the words from Luke 18:

Then He spoke a parable to them, that men always ought to pray and not lose heart, saying: "There was in a certain city a judge who did not fear God nor regard man. Now there was a widow in that city; and she came to him, saying, 'Get justice for me from my adversary.' And he would not for a while; but afterward he said within himself, 'Though I do not fear God nor regard man, yet because this widow troubles me I will avenge her, lest by her continual coming she weary me.'"

Then the Lord said, "Hear what the unjust judge said. And shall God not avenge His own elect who cry out day and night to Him, though He bears long with them? I tell you that He will avenge them speedily. Nevertheless, when the Son of Man comes, will He really find faith on the earth?"

Luke 18:1-8

Clearly, we are not "troubling" the Lord when we ask. Nor is our faith measured by how often we ask. In fact, when I look at the three levels of prayer, I see a progression that keeps going.

Many people fail because their wishbone is where their backbone should be.

Ask. The Bible says in James,

...you do not have because you do not ask. You ask and do not receive, because you ask amiss, that you may spend it on your pleasures.

James 4:2,3

Successful people aren't afraid to ask. And when they ask, they ask the right questions, with the right motives.

Jesus said, "Until now you have not asked for anything in my name. Ask and you will receive, and your joy will be complete" (John 16:24). When was the last time you truly asked the Lord for intervention in your life? You can't get something if you don't ask for it. Asking is the first level of prayer. It's a good starting point for communication with God.

Seek. The next level of prayer is seeking. When you seek God, not only do you vocalize your petition, but you start to move in the direction of the answer. In Christ, there is a 100 percent guarantee. Jesus said,

"...:seek and you will find...."

Matthew 7:7

Those who seek Jesus find Him. There's no frustration, no disappointment. It reminds me of my kids playing hide-and-seek. When my youngest, Jordan, played she would always go hide and wait only a short time before saying, "I'm over here!" She wanted to be found! You need to know that Jesus wants to be found in your life!

Seek the Lord while He may be found, call upon Him while He is near.

Isaiah 55:6

Seek the Lord. Call upon Him. Seeking actually means beating a path to and from. It's going after that which you so desperately need.

It's great to ask God, to petition Him, but when you step up to the level of seeking, you put yourself out in the game—in a place where anything can happen. And when you are working for the Lord and not for man, anything *will* happen!

Knock. The third level of prayer is knocking.

"...knock and the door will be opened to you."

Matthew 7:7

This is the level at which persistence and perseverance kick in. You've asked; then you've put legs to your request and gotten it in

Don't let the delay rob you of the divine.

gear so that action is taking place. Now the asking plus action (seeking) joins with persistence (knocking) in finding that which has been sought. He said He would be found. He even told us when: due season!

*And let us not grow weary while doing good, for **in due season** we shall reap if we do not lose heart.*

Galatians 6:9

There is no "don't season" for those who seek the Lord. It's due time. That's why it's always too soon to quit.

At the knocking level of prayer, you begin to see the doors open and God's favor in your life in ways that can only be described as miraculous. To get to this level of prayer where you knock and doors open, you will need to be persistent.

Calvin Coolidge wrote:

Nothing in the world can take the place of Persistence. Talent will not; nothing is more common than unsuccessful men with talent. Genius will not; unrewarded genius is almost a proverb. Education will not; the world is full of educated derelicts. Persistence and determination alone are omnipotent. The slogan 'Press On' has solved and always will solve the problems of the human race.[3]

The fact is that many people fail because their wishbone is where their backbone should be. They give up too soon, abandoning their dreams and desires.

It's not enough to be a good asker. God isn't the only One responsible for our prayers' being answered. We have some responsibility here too: to seek. And when we seek Him, when we go after Him, His promise is that we will find Him. Then we can boldly knock on the doors that He has always desired to open for us.

What arena of prayer are you operating in? How badly do you want to finish the race, win the prize, and live out your destiny? If you will become an asker, a seeker, and a knocker in prayer, you will become an incredible overcomer for Christ.

That is what the woman with the issue of blood learned.

And He said to her, "Daughter, your faith has made you well. Go in peace, and be healed of your affliction."

Mark 5:34

And that is what Jairus would learn on his journey to destiny. Though it seemed that Jesus was choosing an alternate route, Jairus was not forgotten; his request not ignored.

If you would touch the Healer today, then you, too, would see that He does indeed have time for what is troubling you. Don't let the delay rob you of the divine. Keep asking. Keep seeking. Keep knocking. He's never too busy to stop and heal along the way!

DELAY DISRUPTS THE STADIUM DREAM

When I got back to Tulsa, I called the stadium's general manager to see what we could do. The only day that made sense at every angle was October 22. He informed me that October 22 was set for a Cowboys home game and until everything was final he could not release the date.

Again I was uneasy. Time didn't permit me to wait.

I don't know what it was, but that was the date that felt right in my heart. It felt as if God had scheduled that date for us and the Dallas Cowboys' schedule was the obstacle. At this point of delay, I entered the waiting room of God, trusting Him, praying, and asking Him to make a way where there seemed to be no way.

It was time for the tour to begin, and I had to move ahead with our plans. At this point, you might say I called those things that were not as though they were (Romans 4:17) and penciled the Texas Stadium in on all of the tour calendars for October 22! We even sent out some information to the local area in Dallas to get the promotion going!

Yes, it was risky. Maybe even crazy. I can't tell you I wasn't nervous, but a few facts relieved my doubts. First, I knew that God had placed this dream in Carman's heart. Second, I knew that He'd confirmed it in my heart. Third, I knew that where two or more come together in Jesus' name, He is right there with them. (Matthew 18:20.)

On July 3, I flew back to Tulsa through the Dallas-Fort Worth airport. This was the day the schedules for the National Football League would come out, and I was really sweating it! I felt just like Jairus: Jesus was walking by my side, but we weren't to the house yet! Delay feels awkward, even when Jesus is with you.

EVALUATING YOUR JOURNEY

Season 3: Delays

"I've been waiting my whole life."

"Patience may be a virtue, but I don't have it!"

"Lord, give me patience—and give it to me right now!"

Do any of these phrases sound familiar? Of course they do! We live in a fast-food, convenience store society. Our most popular stores have places for us to eat, to service the car and fill it with gas, to get our groceries, and to buy our lawn supplies—all at the same location. One-stop shopping! Give it to me now!

In this society, the word *delay* can spark a lot of negative feeling. You may feel as if your journey from dreams to destiny has been delayed. As you look at the things that come into your life and seem to hinder your progress in Christ, you may begin to notice a pattern. Perhaps God is refining you to become a better intercessor. Maybe you have become too short-fused and quick-tempered and you just aren't ready to move up to the next level. Whatever the case, as you take some time to reflect on the delays in your life, God will begin to teach you what they mean.

When you hear the word *delay,* what comes into your mind?

_____

_____

_____

_____

_____

_____

_____

_____

_____

_____

_____

_____

List some things in your life right now that you recognize as delays.

_____

_____

_____

_____

_____

_____

_____

_____

_____

_____

_____

_____

_____

_____

God promotes people of character. The German novelist Johann Wolfgang von Goethe said, "You can easily judge the character of a man by how he treats those who can do nothing for him."[4] What does your character say about you today?

_____

_____

_____

_____

_____

_____

_____

_____

_____

_____

_____

_____

_____

_____

_____

_____

_____

_____

_____

_____

_____

_____

_____

_____

_____

_____

_____

_____

_____

_____

The Bible, the book of character, instructs us, "And whatever you do, do it heartily, as to the Lord and not to men knowing that from the Lord you will receive the reward of the inheritance; for you serve the Lord Christ" (Colossians 3:23). What tasks are you currently performing? Which ones are you committing to the Lord? Which ones do you need to commit to Him?

_____

_____

_____

_____

_____

_____

_____

_____

_____

_____

_____

Jesus taught us to ask, seek, and knock in prayer. At which level do you currently pray about your dream? How can you advance to the next level?

_____

_____

_____

_____

_____

_____

_____

_____

_____

_____

_____

_____

_____

_____

One way to successfully go through the season of delay is to focus on the needs of others. Let the Lord lay someone on your heart, and begin to diligently seek the Lord for his or her need. As you focus on intercession for some time, you will become more concerned about others' needs than yours. Then one day you will wake up and find that your needs have been met! Whose needs will you commit to pray for?

_____

_____

_____

_____

_____

_____

_____

_____

_____

_____

What Scriptures will help you grow in character, persistence, and prayer during the season of delay?

_____

_____

_____

_____

_____

_____

_____

_____

_____

_____

_____

_____

_____

Journal your thoughts about delay.

_____

_____

_____

_____

_____

_____

_____

_____

_____

_____

_____

_____

_____

_____

_____

_____

SEASON 4

Divine Assurance

God is ready to interrupt your life right now!

The path from dreams to destiny is not an easy one. Desperation and delay have caused many people to give up on their dreams. But if you don't allow the times of desperation and delay to sabotage your dreams, you're able to move on to the fourth season: the season of divine assurance.

Everyone needs a little help now and then. We all find ourselves in situations that are nearly unbearable, and in those times many of us have tried to cut a deal with God: "God, if You will get me out of this mess, I promise I will _____ (fill in the blank: go to church every week, sing in the choir, go to Sunday school, and so forth)." In those times, what we are seeking is some divine intervention.

The good news is that God is ready to interrupt your life right now! God stands ready to bring you what you need to make it to destiny after the desperation and the delays. He knows where you are in your life right now. He knows what is happening to you, how you feel, and what battles you're facing.

He knew what Jairus was facing too.

DIVINE ASSURANCE REVIVES A FATHER'S DREAM

Jairus had just reached that defining moment when the Lord stopped on the path to His destiny in order to help someone else. All of the emotion Jairus felt, seeing the Lord turn His back away from his daughter and toward someone else, must have been almost too much to bear. Of course we know that the Lord never turns His back on us, but on that day it must have seemed to Jairus that He had.

With every passing moment, Jairus's hope must have waned. His mind called him home to his dying daughter, while his remaining hope for her healing held him firmly by Jesus' side. He must have questioned his determination: "How could I turn my back on my daughter? She needs me; my wife needs me. I shouldn't be here; I should be at home right now." At the same time, he had to have asked himself, "How could I leave our last hope? I have to bring Jesus back with me."

The dream had died. The hope was gone. His worst fears were now reality.

While he stood there waiting as Jesus blessed this newly healed woman, Jairus's head was spinning. Then, suddenly, he recognized familiar voices in the distance. "Jairus!" they called frantically, as the crowd parted to make room for his friends. Then, like a heavy weight, the news broke through Jesus' words and settled into Jairus's mind:

While He was still speaking, some came from the ruler of the synagogue's house who said, "Your daughter is dead. Why trouble the Teacher any further?"

Mark 5:35

The dream had died. The hope was gone. His worst fears were now reality. The pain of those words took his very breath away, and he didn't even have the strength to be angry.

"Why trouble Jesus anymore?" The words clanged in his ears. He'd given it his best shot. He'd run as fast as he could. When he'd found the Healer, he'd thrown his pride and himself at His feet. He'd even held his tongue when Jesus had stopped along the path for a sick woman. He'd done all the right things, but he was too late.

Friend, when you get yourself on the right path and begin to move toward your God-given calling and destiny, you will have times when your dream will seem completely dead. You will experience many highs and many lows. In the good times, you'll know that the Lord is right

It's not your skill that's important; it's His.

there; but in the bad, you may feel as though Jesus has abandoned you and your dream.

Just as they did in Jairus's journey, people will come to you along the way and tell you to give up; they'll tell you to stop troubling the Lord about your dream because it has died. "You'll never be able to have your own ministry," they'll say. Or "You'll never get that job." Or "Why are you starting your own business? You don't have the skill set."

Know this: It's not your skill that's important; it's His. God will develop your skill. God will perfectly equip you for the task at hand, and His grace is always sufficient (just the right amount) for every situation.

"My grace is sufficient for you, for my power is made perfect in weakness."

2 Corinthians 12:9 NIV

The Lord will never forsake you. He knows right where you are. When doubt asks, *Why trouble Jesus anymore?* faith answers: "Because He cares for me. He gave me the dream. He brought me through the desperation and the delays, and He will always complete what He has started."

The Bible promises He will see you through to your destination:

He who began a good work in you will carry it on to completion until the day of Christ Jesus.

Philippians 1:6 NIV

When no one will walk beside you, Jesus will still be there.

The Lord himself goes before you and will be with you; he will never leave you nor forsake you. Do not be afraid; do not be discouraged.

Deuteronomy 31:8 NIV

That's the beauty of this story. Jesus was right there with Jairus when no one else could help him. When his friends brought him word of his daughter's death, his dream's death, his heart flooded with fear.

But then, in Jairus's weakest moment, divine assurance came.

As soon as Jesus heard the word that was spoken, *He said to the ruler of the synagogue, "Do not be afraid; only believe."*

Mark 5:36

Immediately, Jesus responded with hope.

Your words will always disengage your thoughts.

Notice the timing of the Lord: Divine assurance always follows desperation and delay. The Lord is never early, and He is never late. He's always right on time!

Before the negative words had a chance to drop into Jairus's heart, the Lord snatched them back and deactivated them with this simple assurance: "Only believe."

"Only believe" sounds easy, but it requires determination when you're facing severe opposition. If your loved one was sick to the point of death, as Jairus's daughter was, you might hear the words from a friend as encouragement: "Only believe." If you were unemployed for months, someone might say, "Hang in there. Only believe." You may even say it to yourself. If your dream project weren't growing by leaps and bounds, as you thought it would, you may even tell yourself, "Only believe." If the paycheck just doesn't match the expenses and you can't afford to make it another month, you might say, "Only believe."

Belief in these types of situations is rooted in faith in God, as well as an understanding that He is in control. In order to "only believe," you may need to increase your faith and your understanding of God's ability to see you through. Romans 10:17 teaches us how this works:

Faith comes by hearing, and hearing by the word of God.

Because faith comes by hearing the Word of God, your faith will rise to the occasion when you read and meditate on Scripture. Profess the positive Word of God and tell your mind to get in line with your spirit; then let your physical body move forward in the direction of your faith.

Your words will always disengage your thoughts. So if doubt tries to enter your mind, you can immediately stop it with words of faith. This is how you renew your mind to the Word of God, as Romans 12:2 instructs:

> Do not be conformed to this world, but be transformed by
> the renewing of your mind, that you may prove what is
> that good and acceptable and perfect will of God.

When you speak the Word, your ears will hear the Word—and this is how you will build faith and eliminate doubt from your heart. The words from your Sword (the Bible) will cut out the stuff that doesn't belong in your heart, and you will become stronger, healthier, more peaceful, more joyful, and more fulfilled in life. (See Hebrews 4:12.) God's Word helps you become a new person!

Paul wrote about this in his letter to the Ephesians:

> This I say, therefore, and testify in the Lord, that you
> should no longer walk as the rest of the Gentiles walk, in

Sometimes it's best to keep an open mind and a closed mouth—but you'll never need a closed mind and an open mouth.

the futility of their mind, having their understanding darkened, being alienated from the life of God, because of the ignorance that is in them, because of the blindness of their heart; who, being past feeling, have given themselves over to lewdness, to work all uncleanness with greediness.

But you have not so learned Christ, if indeed you have heard Him and have been taught by Him, as the truth is in Jesus: that you put off, concerning your former conduct, the old man which grows corrupt according to the deceitful lusts, and be renewed in the spirit of your mind, and that you put on the new man which was created according to God, in true righteousness and holiness.

Ephesians 4:17-24

When you spend time reading and speaking the Scriptures, your mind changes. One word from God will turn your attitude completely around. Whether you receive that divine assurance through the Scriptures or directly in your heart, it will completely shift your focus back onto God and His ability to see you through.

Lou Holtz said, "Ability is what you are capable of doing. Motivation determines what you do. Attitude determines how well you do it."[5] Getting into the Bible is the quickest way to get an attitude adjustment so you can make it through the delays and disappointments and receive divine assurance on your journey.

Your life tomorrow will be determined by your attitude and choices today.

Your attitude is your point of view. It's what you think and feel, and it affects what you do and say. A lot of people have bad attitudes, and they complain about everyone and everything. I learned a long time ago not to talk about my problems, because 80 percent of people don't care and the other 20 percent think I deserve it! Think before you speak. Sometimes it's best to keep an open mind and a closed mouth—but you'll never need a closed mind and an open mouth (so when your mind goes blank, turn your volume off)!

It's God's plan for you to be made new in your mind so that you can pursue and accomplish His purpose in your life. Your attitude can change not only how you perceive what happens, but also how what happens affects you.

Ultimately, your attitude affects your entire life. William James wrote, "Human beings, by changing the inner attitudes of their minds, can change the outer aspects of their lives."[6] Your life today is a result of your attitude and choices yesterday. Your life tomorrow will be determined by your attitude and choices today.

God wants you to "be renewed in the spirit of your mind." He wants you to change the way you think; to use the mind He gave you for Him. Did you know a cockroach can live nine days without its head before it starves to death? Well, you're not a cockroach. You have to use your head! And you have to use it the way God wants you to if you want to press on to your destiny.

You've probably heard that your attitude determines your altitude. Well, your altitude can also affect your attitude. If you're flying high with God, your perspective changes. This is what divine assurance will do for you. When God speaks into your life—and that often happens directly through the Scriptures—you're not looking at the battle from ground level anymore. You have a bird's eye view, and suddenly you know you can overcome.

Turning your attitude around won't impress the doubters in your life—but it's worth it! Herm Albright wrote, "A positive attitude may not solve all your problems, but it will annoy enough people to make it worth the effort."[7]

What, then, should our attitude be? For the answer, we look to God's Word.

Therefore, since Christ suffered in his body, arm your-
selves also with the same attitude....

1 Peter 4:1 NIV

Our attitude should be that of Christ's. One thing that is true about Christ is that He was a "turnaround specialist."

A man was blind. Jesus turned it around.

Moneychangers were in the temple. He turned it around.

A woman was sick for twelve years. He turned it around.

Unfortunately, if you have the wrong attitude, you can still be considered a turnaround specialist—if you turn around and run! So stop running to God and telling him how big your problem is. He already knows! Start running to your problem and telling it how big your God is! Become a turnaround specialist for Jesus. If you take on the same attitude as Christ, what is there to worry about? Be renewed in the attitude of your mind by digesting the living and active Word of God that judges the thoughts and attitudes of your heart.

Do you want to be a turnaround specialist? To repent means to turn around. Maybe you have been going in the wrong direction for too long. Life is eating you up. Your attitude will be crucial in coming out and finishing your course to destiny. Maybe today you need to change your point of view. Stop being bitter, and start getting better.

You can have the mind and the attitude of Christ. Just ask Him for it. He will teach you to "walk by faith, not by sight" (2 Corinthians 5:7). Then you'll be able to watch God come into your life and conquer your natural limitations, because the supernatural begins where the natural ends. You'll begin to envision the absolute best happening in your life. You'll see the sickness eliminated, the disease destroyed. You'll see yourself with that new job promotion. Even a dead-as-a-rock, dying church will begin to see itself as "living stones...built up a spiritual house, a holy priesthood..." (1 Peter 2:5) when they turn their attitude around and walk by faith.

When your mind, body, and spirit reach this point in the journey, the negative words will no longer impact you because you'll be so filled with the positive Word of God. You'll understand that greater is He that is in you than he that is in the world. (1 John 4:4.) Your spirit will keep your thoughts in check. The peace of God will permit only the things that glorify God and edify you because it will control and rule your heart.

Let the peace of God rule in your hearts, to which also you were called in one body; and be thankful.

Colossians 3:15

God's Word will help you discern the thoughts and intentions of your heart and keep you moving in the right direction.

For the word of God is living and powerful, and sharper than any two-edged sword, piercing even to the division of soul and spirit, and of joints and marrow, and is a discerner of the thoughts and intents of the heart.

Hebrews 4:12

Friends are like an elevator: they will either take you up or they will take you down.

Once you're in agreement with the Word, it's time to change your environment. Look at what Jesus did next on Jairus's journey to destiny. Saying, "Only believe," He prepared to walk with Jairus the rest of the way to his home. However, as Mark 5:37 says,

He permitted no one to follow Him except Peter, James, and John the brother of James.

He only allowed His positive, faithful, tried and true followers to come the rest of the way.

On your journey to destiny, you may need to tell some dream-robbers to go hang around someone else. The Bible says evil company corrupts good habits. (1 Corinthians 15:33.) We can't allow the spirit of criticism and negativity to walk with us on our journey to destiny. Jesus didn't. He sent them away.

I once heard someone say that friends are like an elevator: they will either take you up or they will take you down. We need to be with Spirit-led, Spirit-fed people if we want to go the distance.

Jesus called beside Him those of like faith (2 Peter 1:1), and with Jairus they proceeded to walk out of the natural and into the supernatural. Many people don't make it to the *supernatural* because their companions hold them back in the *natural.* Many stay in the natural because they're afraid to lose control. These people seek natural comfort rather than the supernatural Comforter. They lack trust, and ultimately they doubt everything and everybody.

Doubt opposes everything we need on our journey to destiny. Doubt comes from fear, and fear is the devil's greatest weapon against our efforts to move forward. Fear doesn't come from God. Second Timothy 1:7 says:

For God has not given us a spirit of fear, but of power and of love and of a sound mind.

As God's children, we have to recognize that we are filled with a spirit of power, love, and a sound mind. We can't allow fear and doubt to grasp our minds. Doubt has no benefits. Doubters are on the outside of the supernatural realm, never experiencing the miraculous power of the Lord.

Doubters simply cannot "Only believe," but believers can. On your journey from dreams to destiny, find people who will believe with you that the desires of your heart will be fulfilled. Pray together, eat together, play together, and watch your attitude begin to change as you stir up one another to do good works, as Hebrews 10:24 says:

When you've received assurance from the Lord, nothing will stop you.

> *Let us consider one another in order to stir up love and good works, not forsaking the assembling of ourselves together, as is the manner of some, but exhorting one another, and so much the more as you see the Day approaching.*

When you assemble with those of like, precious faith, soon you'll begin to see the delivering power of God manifested in each other's lives. You'll begin to recognize how far you have journeyed with God and how close you've come to your divine destiny.

Jairus, alongside Jesus, Peter, James, and John, was on his way to divine destiny. When he'd needed it most, he'd heard the divine assurance of the Lord. God always delivers when we trust Him. Jesus' words "Only believe" had quickened his spirit, and the faith-filled crew marched on toward his home.

As they walked, the drone of the crowd began to fade and another sound began to reach them. The noise of wailing mourners filled the dry air as they came near the house. Though Jairus was aware that this mourning was for his daughter, he somehow knew something good was coming.

Jesus was by his side.

It will happen for you, too, on your journey from dreams to destiny. The Lord will say to you, "Do not be afraid; only believe!" Then, with the Lord's assurance, your spirit will rise up within you and you'll feel a second wind of enthusiasm and excitement about your dream. You'll start believing that your dream is actually becoming your destiny, just as the Lord said it would when He planted the vision inside you.

When you've received assurance from the Lord, nothing will stop you. Your attitude will be unaffected by the natural situation, the mourning doubters. You'll know you're moving in the right direction, with the right crowd, and best of all with Jesus right beside you!

DIVINE ASSURANCE RESTORES
THE STADIUM DREAM

I walked over to the *Dallas Morning News* counter to get the paper, opened up the sports section, and looked for the newly released Dallas Cowboys football schedule. I needed to see an opening for our concert on October 22, but I knew it would take a miracle for it to happen. It took my eyes forever to scroll through all the dates: August pre-season . . . September . . . October 1 . . . 8 . . . 15 . . . 22. My eyes blurred, then focused.

The Cowboys were playing on the 22.

But they were in Arizona against the Cardinals!

I know I screamed right there in the airport. I'm sure I looked like a lottery winner! I smiled and grabbed my cell phone to call the stadium's general manager to wrap things up.

That day I knew all about divine assurance and divine intervention. Our dream wouldn't die. We were on our way home with Jesus by our side!

It's hard to beat the feeling I had that day as I finished my flight to Tulsa, knowing everything was sealed shut and ready to go. All that was left was a complete mail-out to our partner list and some radio time. After that, God would have to take care of bringing the people.

If it were easy to do, everyone would be doing it. It's only impossible until somebody does it!

August and September seemed to last forever. Waiting for that concert was worse than waiting for ketchup to come out of the bottle. We could feel the anticipation, but we'd just have to wait for that divine date.

The budget for the stadium event kept growing. More and more unforeseen expenses arose, and the final tally was more than $372,000! In the past, I'd agreed in faith with Carman for many things, but we'd never needed to believe for this much money.

I remember Carman calling in August and asking if we were about to make the biggest mistake of our lives. We were both nervous.

It was risky.

It was beyond what we could do.

But that's what God desired! You see, it wasn't about us; it was about Him!

Carman and I were a good support system for each other. I tried to be encouraging to Carman, and when I was down Carman had the right words for me. I guess that's why Jesus sent the disciples out in twos— so they could spur each other on, especially when things got tough. (Mark 6:7.) We supported each other continually, but the traumas weren't over yet.

Early in the week of our performance, we pulled in to Dallas with a huge budget, a large crew of helpers, and unsettled spirits. Several of my peers called that week to unload their dockets of doubt. One record executive, expecting about 25,000 people to show up, asked me how I could set Carman up for embarrassment like this. He had a point. When you're working with a $372,000 budget and a 70,000-seat venue, his estimated crowd of 25,000 *would* look a bit ridiculous.

Then the week of the concert arrived, and we began setting up. Now, keep in mind that Texas Stadium has a big hole—almost the size of Texas—in the top of it. Monday the rains began. Well, *rains* is an under-statement. Water in Noah's Ark-like proportions fell from the sky. As you'd imagine, it wasn't easy to set up that week! But if it were easy to do, everyone would be doing it. It's only impossible until somebody does it!

In the middle of the rainstorm, we had to start rigging—hanging our sound and lights from the ceiling of the stadium. With my rigging crew hanging on the beam crossing the roof of the stadium, the lightning started. It was unbelievable! Tuesday, Wednesday, and Thursday looked the same, and we were falling behind schedule.

Then the stadium engineers showed up to tell us our speakers weighed too much to hang on the beams. Our concert was done in the round, with the stage in the center and chairs all around it. No one had ever done this at Texas Stadium before, and the stadium engineers decided our plan and the hanging weight would all have to change.

I ran from the production office to the field where the engineers, tour production manager, and rigging crew were, and we started to look at the blueprints. I was already exhausted. There were so many things to deal with here that had never needed to be addressed in our events before. Things like twenty-five different areas on three different stadium levels to sell T-shirts and CDs. Tarps that came in from Houston to cover the field. Plywood sheets to lay on top of the turf to protect it from damage. Generators for power, because we couldn't use the power available at the stadium.

I answered, or at least tried to answer, more questions that week than I had in my entire lifetime up till that point.

I realized something that week: Everything *is* big in Texas! Even the work!

Thursday night in a TV appearance, Carman announced that 65,000 people would be at Texas Stadium on Saturday evening. Talk about pressure! I was feeling every bit of it!

Friday morning started with breakfast in preparation for two in-store appearances in the Dallas area. Carman could meet people, sign some CDs, and promote this event. It was becoming more ominous now as the moment approached, and sometimes I had to sit and say nothing because my nerves were shell-shocked.

The first store was in Plano. On the way, I got my chance to ask Carman what had possessed him to say that 65,000 would be at the concert. He smiled. That's all he did! I guess it was faith that rose up in him. Sometimes faith makes you say things you would never say on your own.

Now I *really* felt the pressure! My buddies were expecting 25,000 people, and Carman was looking for 65,000! And then there was that looming $372,000 needed to pay the bills!

Once again, I found myself going back to what God had said and done to bring us to this point in the journey. Sometimes that's all you can do.

I remembered Jairus waiting for Jesus to heal the woman with the issue of blood, only to see the mourners running from his house to tell him to forget about trying anymore; his little girl was dead. "Why bother Jesus?" they'd shouted.

My "mourners" would shout through the car radio minutes later: "The storms have caused some tornadoes to start, and the winds have torn paneling off of homes a mile away from Texas Stadium." This was too much! *God, didn't You say You wouldn't give us more than we could bear?* I prayed silently, remembering 1 Corinthians 10:13.

Despite the weather, the store appearances were great. The people were so kind, but no one knew what was happening behind the scenes.

EVALUATING YOUR JOURNEY

Season 4: Divine Assurance

When you start pursuing your dream, when you get through the desperation and find yourself waiting in the season of delay, you will arrive at a place where you need encouragement. You will need things to start to line up for your benefit to give you your second wind so you can make it to the finish line of your destiny. You will need to know that everything will be okay. What you'll need then is divine assurance.

In business contracts people ask for assurances, or points that they want to be guaranteed for them. When God comes through with divine assurance for you, He guarantees the success of your dream. It feels as if your world has just settled into the place where it's always needed to be.

Faith is what will get you through this season until your destiny is fulfilled. Believe in your dream, in the One who put it in you, and in His ability to walk you through to your destiny. Make an effort to find some time to be still before the Lord and listen for His divine directives before taking the next steps. When you don't know what to do, sometimes it's best to do nothing. Tell yourself that you won't move until you know God is moving with you.

Have you ever felt the Lord speaking to you? How did it make you feel, and what happened in your life as a result?

_____

_____

_____

_____

_____

_____

_____

_____

_____

_____

_____

_____

_____

_____

_____

_____

When you're waiting for divine assurance, it helps to go back and recapture the feelings you had when you began your journey to destiny. In the beginning, what thoughts inspired you to start pursuing your dream?

_____

_____

_____

_____

_____

_____

_____

_____

_____

_____

_____

_____

_____

If God intervened in your life in a mighty way today, what would that look like? What would happen for you?

_____

_____

_____

_____

_____

_____

_____

_____

_____

_____

_____

_____

_____

_____

Who are your faithful friends who can walk with you to the fulfillment of your dream?

_____

_____

_____

_____

_____

_____

_____

_____

_____

_____

_____

_____

_____

_____

Who are the doubters in your life who, at this time, will not be able to make the journey with you to your destiny?

_____

_____

_____

_____

_____

_____

_____

_____

_____

_____

_____

_____

_____

_____

_____

_____

_____

_____

_____

_____

_____

_____

_____

_____

_____

_____

_____

_____

_____

_____

_____

There is tremendous power in your testimony, and you need to share your victories and successes up to this point with others. The word of your testimony is a powerful weapon over all the evil that comes against you. (Revelation 12:11.) What are some of the key points of your testimony that you can share with others to ignite their faith and rekindle your own?

You will also need an arsenal of Scripture to combat the negative forces that will bombard you as you determine to reach your destiny. Start standing on the Word of God and speaking His promises, for each one is "yes" and "amen" to the believer. (2 Corinthians 1:20.) List the Scriptures that have helped you through the desperation and delays, and begin to speak them every day as you complete your journey.

What assures you that your dreams will come to pass?

_____

_____

_____

_____

_____

_____

_____

_____

_____

_____

_____

_____

_____

_____

_____

Journal your thoughts about divine assurance.

_____

_____

_____

_____

_____

_____

_____

_____

_____

_____

_____

_____

_____

_____

_____

SEASON 5

Destiny Fulfilled!

Destiny is that which is certain to happen in the future.

The Olympic Games. Mexico. 1968. The marathon is the final event on the program. The Olympic stadium is packed, and excitement builds as the first athlete, an Ethiopian runner, enters the stadium. The crowd erupts as he crosses the finish line.

Way back in the field is another runner, John Stephen Akwhari of Tanzania. He has been eclipsed by the other runners. After thirty kilometers his head is throbbing, his muscles are aching, and he falls to the ground. He has serious leg injuries and officials want him to retire, but he refuses. With his knee bandaged, Akwhari picks himself up and hobbles the remaining 12 kilometers to the finish line. An hour after the winner has finished, Akwhari enters the stadium. All but a few thousand of the crowd have gone home. Akwhari moves around the track at a painstakingly slow pace, until finally he collapses over the finish line.

It is one of the most heroic efforts of Olympic history. Afterward, asked by a reporter why he didn't drop out, Akwhari says, "My country did not send me to start the race. They sent me to finish."

Somewhere in your past, you made the decision to chart out a course, to start the training regimen and run the race in such a way as to get the prize. The journey from dreams to destiny is like a marathon: It's not how you start that counts, but rather how you finish. A marathon journey may seem impossible to you, but you will make it step by step with Jesus by your side. Inch by inch, everything's a cinch. You will make it to your destiny when you think like this.

Destiny is that which *is certain to happen* in the future. You can be sure of it. Destiny is the season you envision, pray for, and persevere for. It's where you long to be, and it's where you will be when you have patiently continued and have asked, sought, and knocked on Jesus' door in prayer. When you near your destiny, you'll know that your perseverance will soon be rewarded. You'll feel like a runner in the final mile of the marathon, the winning team in the last minute of the championship game, the new parents in the moments before their child is born. You'll be getting ready for the victory celebration!

People will make fun of you as you pursue your dreams.

That's how Jairus felt when he came near his house.

DESTINY FULFILLED FOR
A FATHER'S DREAM

As Jairus came over the final hill before reaching his home, his pace must have quickened. His spirit must have been so filled with determination that he didn't even hear the mourners still wailing in his house. He was ready for a miracle. The miracle-worker Himself and His entourage walked right beside him.

I imagine Jairus arriving at the door one step ahead of Jesus, anticipating what would come. Then, amid the loud mourners, I see Jesus, the Prince of Peace, entering the home where the dream was born. Suddenly the crying stopped. The noise was silenced. Every head turned toward the door, and every eye fixed on the famed miracle-worker.

Then Jesus spoke: "Why all the commotion and weeping? The girl isn't dead; she's sleeping."

Then He came to the house of the ruler of the synagogue,
and saw a tumult and those who wept and wailed loudly.
When He came in, He said to them, "Why make this
commotion and weep? The child is not dead, but sleeping."

Mark 5:38,39

But the mourners ridiculed Him. (v. 40.) They couldn't understand this supernatural realm, and they laughed at Him.

Choose carefully the people you share your journey with.

Friend, if they made fun of Jesus, be certain that people will make fun of you as you pursue your dreams. Some people just don't have faith for the miracle, even when the miracle-worker is standing right in front of them. This is why it's so important to surround yourself with the right people.

Despite the mourners, Jairus's heart must have smiled when the Lord said his daughter was only sleeping. He must have looked like the dad watching his son score the winning run of the Little League All-Star game or the dad watching his little girl graduate from college. There's no other feeling like it: excitement, anticipation, accomplishment, and joy all wrapped up in one.

Jesus grabbed the hands of Jairus and his wife and motioned to Peter, James, and John to come with Him. The ones left behind were the mourners, those who could not believe.

> And they ridiculed Him. But when He had put them all outside, He took the father and the mother of the child, and those who were with Him, and entered where the child was lying.

Mark 5:40

Jesus only took Peter, James, John, Jairus and his wife into the room of the little girl. I believe God wants to put encouragers in your path, too. It's important to Him to see the right people walking with you to your destiny. In order to make it to your destiny, you need to surround yourself with those who are truly faithful and can connect with God in prayer. It matters to God, and it should matter to you!

Everyone else in Jairus's house was so full of doubt that they'd laughed at Jesus when He'd said the little girl was simply sleeping. People will laugh at you, too, and try to discredit your dreams—so choose carefully the people you share your journey with. It's time to stop listening to the doubters. The transition may be gradual, but it's necessary if you want to walk into your destiny.

As they opened the door to the room where the little girl lay, I believe Jesus stopped for a brief moment, looked straight into her parents' eyes, and smiled as if to say, "Everything is going to work out fine. Your faith in Me has brought you to this point, and it will bring you to your destiny."

Then Jesus approached the little girl lying on her bed.

Then He took the child by the hand, and said to her, "Talitha, cumi," which is translated, "Little girl, I say to you, arise." Immediately the girl arose and walked, for she was twelve years of age. And they were overcome with great amazement.

Mark 5:41,42

Jesus said, "Little girl, I say to you, 'Arise!'" Immediately, her little eyes opened and she got up from the bed and started walking around. The dream was alive! Everyone in the room was filled with amazement.

Jairus had made it to the end of the roller coaster ride and saw his little girl healed. Though he'd felt a plethora of emotions along the way, he'd remained close to Jesus and never left His side. When the situation had seemed out of control and he was desperate, he'd asked, sought, and knocked at Jesus' door to receive His help. When he could have gotten angry and stormed off because of the delays, he'd patiently continued with Jesus. When he could have given up on faith and acknowledged the negative feelings, he'd listened to Jesus' divine assurance and determined to "only believe." Finally, at the end of that miraculous day, Jesus entered his home and Jairus rejoiced with Him as his dream came back to life.

DESTINY MEETS
THE STADIUM DREAM

Friday night arrived, and Carman and I went for a jog. We liked to do that—or at least *he* did because he could outrun me. While we were running Carman received a phone call from the guy who'd started all of this—the one who'd seen something in Carman that no one else had, the one who'd believed when no one else had. It was Jimmy Bowen.

During that conversation, I could see Carman begin to relax. Mr. Bowen had no idea that God was using him as oxygen to inflate the soul of the man who would stand on the stage Saturday night to tell people about Jesus Christ. When that call was over, Carman looked different. His countenance had changed. He ran, and he ran, and he ran. He became Forrest Gump!

Friday night I don't think I slept at all. The rain was still coming down, and it easily could have ruined everything. (Remember: There's a huge hole in the top of Texas Stadium!) Tired and irritated, I wondered, *Why couldn't we have chosen a stadium totally shielded from the elements?* This week had been an emotional roller coaster, but it was almost over. I'd only made it this far by going back to what God had said and done in this journey from a dream to destiny. Sometimes that's all you can do.

Saturday Morning, 6 A.M., October 22, 1994

Maybe I dozed off for an hour that night, but bright and early I was up and running to the window to pull back the curtains. I was nervous, curious—and excited. As I threw open the curtain, the sun was already shining as if God was saying, "Here it is! I saved it for today, so go and do what I prepared you to do!"

Now the butterflies started to flutter as we made the final preparations. At this point, there wasn't very much we could do to change the outcome. We were at that place where, having done all we could do, we just had to stand and trust God. (Ephesians 6:13.) It must have been how Jairus felt standing at the edge of his daughter's bed as the Master approached, ready to heal her. All Jairus could do was stand there. That was all I could do, too. It was out of my hands.

The rest of the day was a blur. The phone and two-way radios were buzzing all day, my family and friends were in town, and everyone was in awe of the magnitude of this day. It was finally here. We were in Texas Stadium.

Oh yes, and we'd already spent $372,000.

That monetary detail alone would have been enough to cause those butterflies to multiply. But amazingly, while I planned the details of this outreach, I never even thought about the budget. I was so busy doing my part that the detours were not even an issue. There were no distractions now. I was "in the zone," totally focused for such a time as this. (See Esther 4:14.)

As the afternoon progressed, the excitement increased. It was almost time to open the doors. Little did I know it, but another challenge lay ahead.

5:30 P.M., October 22: D-Day!

It was D-Day, Destiny Day, and the moment had arrived to open the doors to the public. Nothing else could be changed. Now we would just have to fix trouble as it arrived—and it would continue arriving all night.

As the doors opened, I monitored everything that I could, circling the stadium in a golf cart. Texas Stadium was more like the Texas Motor Speedway for me that night as I bounced from end to end putting out the small fires, answering questions, and keeping Carman informed of the crowd control.

One of the greatest churches in Texas was helping us under the leadership of a wonderful friend of mine, John Jonas. He'd been instrumental in gathering over 3,000 people who offered themselves as a living sacrifice unto God and helped us to be as hospitable as possible to the crowd. (See Romans 12:1.) They greeted, offered directions, sold T-shirts, passed out information, and demonstrated Jesus to everyone who entered the gates.

People came in for over an hour. It was amazing. They settled into all the areas of the facility. Some went to the top, maybe for a bird's-eye view, while others went to the field level. The police were keeping me informed of the traffic coming in on all five arteries of highway leading to the stadium. The stadium was swelling, and people were buzzing with excitement. In all of

This wasn't the picture of my dream.

the anticipation and attention to detail, I was about to get the shock of my life. It was just after 7 P.M. when I received the latest update from the police.

Every report up till this time had been that the roads were full of cars and people were steadily coming in—but this report was different.

The highways were clear.

The gates were no longer packed with people.

I went back into the stadium and looked at the people.

There seemed to be about 40,000.

My heart sank. I felt like I would be sick.

I stalled radioing Carman to let him know what the police had told me.

All the people are in, I thought. *This is it. Are all my peers right? Is it over?*

You'd think that with 40,000 people screaming and looking for an experience with Christ, I would have been elated. But this wasn't the picture of my dream. This wasn't what Carman had seen, and this wasn't what I wanted.

When I finally radioed Carman, I could feel his disappointment too. It's hard to look at your dream if the picture isn't what you were seeing in your heart. No one tells you what to do with those kinds of feelings. There's no seminar on dealing with hope deferred, and it does just what the Bible says it does: it makes your heart hurt. (Proverbs 13:12.)

I never gave in to the idea that all the doubters were right and God was wrong.

My next job would be to go to the stage to tell the people that everyone was there. I'd have to tell everyone in the upper deck to come down to another level so the volunteers at the top could be released from service. This would make the event more manageable for our crew and keep our costs down.

I was angry. I didn't want to go to the stage and give this announcement. I felt like I was giving in, and this was not what I'd signed up for. I felt stupid. I felt like I had failed.

I'm almost positive this was how Isaac felt as he prepared to kill his son as a sacrifice to God. (See Genesis 22.) This couldn't be God. How could I kill my dream?

Reluctantly, I made my way to the stage and made the announcement. I was praying all the way and, honestly, my prayer was not full of faith but was mixed with anger. I was a child who'd not received what he felt his Father had promised, so I let Him hear it.

And hear it He did.

Though I was disappointed and angry, I never gave in to the idea that all the doubters were right and God was wrong. I stood by the dream He'd given us.

And so did He. He'd stood by Isaac and held back his hand from destroying his son, his dream. Now He stood by me and preserved the dream He'd given us.

Within twenty minutes, the crowd control personnel called me. More people were coming! More people were on the interstate. Someone had opened the floodgates, and people were pouring on to the property and coming through the gates. I'd never seen anything like it! Father God had given a gift to His sons! The gates were packed, and a steady stream of people made their way into the building. There were another 10,000, then 10,000 more—and they just kept coming. We were running out of room! Now what would we do?

The police started telling folks bottlenecked on the five highways into Irving to turn around and go home. They were amazed when the people told them, "God bless you!" and left peacefully. The police told us they'd never seen people acting so nice after being told to go home.

The people kept coming until 71,102 of them made it in and we had to close the doors. It was truly spectacular! You know that I was smiling from ear to ear now. God had smiled on us, and life was good.

The next time I took the stage to welcome the people, my attitude was different. I even decided to tell a joke, but I was a bit scared when the only response was silence. Four seconds later, the laughter rang out. It had taken that long for the response to get back to the stage. What an amazing experience! I was feeling great now, watching a dream become destiny.

One thing I learned from this test is how important it is to have people surrounding you who are called in their profession.

8 P.M., October 22: Show Time!

There's no other feeling in the world like standing by a stage as excitement builds and the lights go out. On that October night in Texas, 71,102 screams filled that legendary stadium. Then, when the lights went out, the volume doubled.

But there would be one more test.

Normally, the lights are only off for a brief moment. When the music starts, the musicians take their places and the lights come back on. But on this night, the stadium was pitch black, the people were screaming, and it seemed to take forever for the music to start.

What was going on?

Our program had been synchronized. The lights, music, and video images all ran together in sync. When something happened to one, it happened to them all. Our system had frozen, so nothing was coming on. The lights wouldn't operate, and everyone was screaming!

One thing I learned from this test is how important it is to have people surrounding you who are called in their profession. Carman Ministries had experts in their field: the best lighting and sound people, the most gifted dancers and musicians; at the helm was Carman, one of the most charismatic and anointed people in the musical world.

As Carman stood on the side of the stage waiting, we were in lock-down. This was where our crews' gifts would shine. All of our technical people jumped right in to figure out the problem. Though the situation seemed desperate, it was only a matter of seconds before they'd unlocked the system and we were rolling!

I believe that if we hadn't had all the previous years of preparation, the right people in the right places, and the anointing of God on us, we may never have gotten that concert going. But God knew that night would come, and He'd led us every step of the way.

The music started, the video kicked in, and the dancers and musicians took the stage in the most incredible concert experience we'd ever been a part of. The people were still screaming, and then Carman walked out onto the stage.

History was made. It was the largest Christian concert by a solo artist, and that night over 5,000 people received Christ for the first time.

To this day, I can still feel the emotions that ran through my being during that incredible event. It was astonishing then, and is even today, to think that God would allow me to experience His awesome power, and play a role in His touching lives and bringing people into a relationship with Him in such a magnificent way. I was honored to be part of His story in history. Garth Brooks may have friends in low places, but I'm thankful I've got friends in high places!

WHAT ABOUT THAT $372,000 BILL?

One other amazing miracle occurred for us as we moved toward the completion of this historic concert date in Texas. As you will recall, the budget was $372,000. Now, even with the building full of people, statistically we would either come in right on budget or be a little bit short. Approaching the concert date, we had tabulated all of the monies that had come in from our partners to produce this event. Even with an offering similar to the ones we'd received on the rest of the tour dates, and even if we sold boxes and boxes of T-shirts, we would fall short of this budget. It was just too much money.

That afternoon, as I was feeling the pressure and the magnitude of this event, I received a phone call from an incredible organization that was part of our volunteer crew for the stadium event. The Fellowship of Christian Athletes (FCA) was planning a big party for Tom Landry's seventieth birthday, and wanted to have it in the stadium on Sunday.

The problem was that our equipment and stage would not be out of the building in time. For a concert this size, it would take a couple days to get everything out. The FCA had already confirmed an incoming flight for Louise Mandrell to sing, and many VIPs were participating.

I wasn't prepared for their question: "Could we use your lights, sound, and stage? Would you leave them up another night for, say, a donation to Carman Ministries of $50,000?"

That was just about how much we needed to break even on the concert! I can't tell you just how big God was to me as we confirmed that deal.

What an amazing event! What a concert! What a God! And He just kept the miracles coming. It was truly supernatural!

EVALUATING YOUR JOURNEY

Season 5: Destiny Fulfilled!

Destiny feels like scoring the winning run in the All-Star game, receiving a standing ovation after singing a song, or accepting an award for an incredible accomplishment. There's nothing like it. And the beautiful truth is that all of the dreams God gives you will turn to destiny if you continue with Him in the journey.

When you successfully journey through the five seasons and fulfill a dream, take time to acknowledge the incredible achievement that God has enabled you to experience. Take a moment today to reflect upon the journey you've been taking as a follower of the Lord. Notice the spiritual landmarks and milestones that you've crossed, and keep them close to you as a memorial of what the Lord has done.

What has God enabled you to achieve on your journey from dreams to destiny?

Have you reached your destiny? What does it look like?

_____

_____

_____

_____

_____

_____

_____

_____

_____

_____

_____

_____

_____

_____

_____

Whether you're still on your path to destiny, or you've fulfilled one dream, start praying for someone else's dreams to be fulfilled. The Bible says we are to pray one for another that we may be healed. (James 5:16.) As you esteem your brothers' and sisters' needs above your own, you position yourself for your own miracles. Whose needs will you pray for this week?

_____

_____

_____

_____

_____

_____

_____

_____

_____

_____

_____

Journal your thoughts about destiny.

_____

_____

_____

_____

_____

_____

_____

_____

_____

_____

_____

_____

_____

_____

_____

A New Dream

There's a
difference
between
being full
and being
fulfilled.

There is nothing as sweet as the birth of a newborn child. Those tiny little hands, the cooing, the soft skin. But at the eleventh hour, when Mom is screaming like she's being controlled by a demonic force, you might doubt the outcome. Turning dreams to destiny is like that. It's a birthing process. It's fun in the beginning and at the completion—but most of us, given the choice, would opt out of all that stuff in the middle.

People who make it from dreams to destiny understand that the process is not an easy one, but that they can make it with the Lord by their side. They know that the joy of the Lord is their strength. (Nehemiah 8:10.) They know that, through the desperation and the delays, a merry heart does good like a medicine. (Proverbs 17:22.)

Have you ever laughed when things were bad—perhaps because they were *so* bad you couldn't even believe it and you just had to laugh? That's not being ignorant; that is the Spirit of God taking over and responding with strength to your weakness.

And He said to me, "My grace is sufficient for you, for My strength is made perfect in weakness."

2 Corinthians 12:9

Philippians 4:4 says, "Rejoice in the Lord always. Again I will say, rejoice!" It takes fourteen muscles to smile and seventy-two to frown. Maybe that's why so many people are always tired! The Bible says we're supposed to rejoice in the Lord. And just to be sure we get the point, the verse says it again: "rejoice!" Rejoice always and in all ways, and all that energy and strength will be restored to you so that you can continue the journey and fulfill your dreams.

People who reach their destiny know that being teachable is the only way to make it.

People who've made it through the five seasons know that availability is more important than ability.

I beseech you therefore, brethren, by the mercies of God, that you present your bodies a living sacrifice, holy, acceptable to God, which is your reasonable service.

Romans 12:1

Being available is an act of worship. Sometimes you say, "I just have no money to invest in what God is doing." Then invest yourself. You are your greatest resource. The body of Christ needs people who are available! People who present themselves to God, who make themselves available to Him, become the testimony of His dreams fulfilled.

People who reach their destiny know that being teachable is the only way to make it. Proverbs 12:1 says, "Whoever loves instruction loves knowledge, but he who hates correction is stupid." A meek spirit is a teachable spirit, and Jesus said, "Blessed are the meek, for they shall inherit the earth" (Matthew 5:5). When you are teachable, doors will open up for you.

It is the Holy Spirit who will teach you and lead you on your path to destiny.

"But the Helper, the Holy Spirit, whom the Father will send in My name, He will teach you all things, and bring to your remembrance all things that I said to you. Peace I leave with you, My peace I give to you; not

One of the secrets to achievement in God is to not let what you're doing get to you before you get to it.

139

as the world gives do I give to you. Let not your heart be troubled, neither let it be afraid."

John 14:26,27

The Holy Spirit reminds you what you have learned from Scripture, and He confirms the peace that you were given. He helps you distinguish between God's peace and the world's peace, and He teaches you how to let His peace rule.

Let the peace of Christ rule in your hearts, since as members of one body you were called to peace. And be thankful.

Colossians 3:15 NIV

One of the secrets to achievement in God is to not let what you're doing get to you before you get to it. And when you do get to it, get to it with all your heart. Pour yourself into it. You may get your heart stomped, broken, or bruised—but you will not be defeated! Peace will control your heart when, through the desperation and the delays, you have a thankful heart and when the Word dwells in you. You will make it to your destiny!

When it's all said and done, if you will pursue God, "you will find Him if you seek Him with all your heart and with all your soul" (Deuteronomy 4:29).

The truth of this Scripture was evident in Jairus's life as he watched his dream become his destiny and new dreams being born.

If you don't feed your dreams, they'll die.

A NEW CHAPTER BEGINS IN A FATHER'S NEW DREAM

As Jairus held his daughter in his arms after her miraculous resurrection, his eyes must have flooded with tears. He must have sensed the arms of God wrapped around his whole family, and all of his dreams revived. The girl who had just lain at death's door now, with the beautiful color of life in her cheeks, walked toward Jesus to embrace her Healer. Once again, the dream of her wedding day captured Jairus's heart and he knew she would one day become the woman he was destined to train her to be.

After the little girl stood up and walked, Jesus told her parents to give her something to eat.

But He commanded them strictly that no one should know it, and said that something should be given her to eat.

Mark 5:43

Eventually, everyone would know what had happened to this young girl, but right now Jesus wanted to focus on her needs. He didn't send someone out to announce the miracle. She didn't need a crowd of people around her. We don't know how long she'd been sick, but she was well now and needed nourishment to regain her strength.

Did the Lord give you a dream that seems to have died? When you bring Jesus to the dream He gave you and allow Him to touch it and bless it, it will live and everyone around you will be amazed. The Lord will be glorified through your victory.

Then you, too, will need to feed your dreams. Continually give them the bread of life and allow them to grow.

> *And Jesus said to them, "I am the bread of life. He who comes to Me shall never hunger, and he who believes in Me shall never thirst."*
>
> John 6:35

If you don't feed your dreams, they'll die. When your dreams start to fade, you need to feed them Jesus' words of clarity and vision. When you face seasons of desperation and delay, you have to feed your dreams Jesus' words of hope and faith. When it seems that you've been waiting forever for your dreams to grow and nothing is happening, feed them Jesus' words of life.

Highlight in your Bible the Scriptures the Lord has told you to stand upon as you pursue your destiny. Repeat these words of life to yourself until you feel faith rising up within your heart and doubt disappearing. As you feed your dreams God's promises, you will see them grow.

Then, when you have walked a dream through to destiny, you, too, will find old dreams revived and new dreams born in your heart. The Christian walk is always progressive, and you will always find fresh new ways to use your gifts to bless others and glorify Jesus. As you continue on your journey from dreams to destiny, the Lord will plant big dreams in your heart and motivate you to become more than a conqueror in every area of your life. (Romans 8:37.)

When you pursue God, you make your way to a place that God has already carved out for you. It's your own personal niche. The reward of finding that place is being in the perfect will of God for your life, working for the Lord and not for man.

Whatever you do, work at it with all your heart, as working for the Lord, not for men.

Colossians 3:23 NIV

As a follower of Christ, you will serve people in some capacity. However, even if you're serving people, remember that you are ultimately serving the Lord. And remember that He is the One providing you with the ability to do it. According to Romans 12:6-8, serving people is a spiritual gift.

If your gift is that of serving others, serve them well.

Romans 12:7

_____

Many people start to serve and then stop abruptly because they don't understand the source of the ability to serve. They don't know that serving is a gift from God. If you know that you're called to serve, you don't grow weary in well doing. It's like marriage. When you make a commitment, even if you want to break it sometimes, you just won't quit.

People who won't quit but continue serving understand the importance of receiving motivation from the Spirit within. There is a growing need in our culture today to understand and tap into the secret of motivation. Motivation is that which causes action. It determines what you do—and *do* you must. You may be on the right track, but if you don't move forward you'll get run over by the train.

All of us are motivated by what we see, hear, taste, smell, and feel. All five senses are involved in determining what we do with our time, effort, and energy.

It's a constant struggle to maintain our motivation.

What advertisers have realized, what songwriters know, and what retail stores understand is that *we want to be moved*. We like certain songs because they appeal to our hearing. Images on our TV and computer screens appeal to our sight. We

144

pay motivational speakers big money to appeal to our senses and ignite that thing within us that will cause us to move.

It's a constant struggle to maintain our motivation. Paul recognized that in his own life.

I'm not saying that I have this all together, that I have it made. But I am well on my way, reaching out for Christ, who has so wondrously reached out for me. Friends, don't get me wrong: By no means do I count myself an expert in all of this, but I've got my eye on the goal, where God is beckoning us onward—to Jesus. I'm off and running, and I'm not turning back.

So let's keep focused on that goal, those of us who want everything God has for us. If any of you have something else in mind, something less than total commitment, God will clear your blurred vision—you'll see it yet! Now that we're on the right track, let's stay on it.

Philippians 3:12-16 MESSAGE

Paul's motivation was the prize at the end of the race. For this, he would never let his eyes wander or his motivation fade. This should be our motivation as well.

God has
given us a
Book full of
motivation.

In the Word, God gave us many instructions using our five senses to help us stay motivated.

For the sense of sight, for example, He gave us Hebrews 12:2:

Looking unto Jesus, the author and finisher of our faith, who for the joy that was set before Him endured the cross, despising the shame, and has sat down at the right hand of the throne of God.

For the sense of hearing, He gave us James 1:19:

So then, my beloved brethren, let every man be swift to hear, slow to speak, slow to wrath....

And for hearing, He gave us these words of wisdom:

The way of a fool seems right to him, but a wise man listens to advice.

Proverbs 12:15 NIV

For the sense of taste, He gave us Proverbs 24:13-14:

My son, eat honey because it is good, and the honeycomb
which is sweet to your taste; so shall the knowledge of
wisdom be to your soul.

Joshua 1:8, though it may not appear so at first glance, appeals to our sense of taste because the word *meditate* actually refers to a cow chewing its cud.

This Book of the Law shall not depart from your mouth,
but you shall meditate in it day and night, that you may
observe to do according to all that is written in it. For then
you will make your way prosperous, and then you will
have good success.

In 2 Corinthians, He appeals to the sense of smell:

For we are to God the fragrance of Christ among those
who are being saved and among those who are perishing.

God has given us a Book full of motivation because He wants our lives to be motivated by Him and by His Word on our journey from dreams to destiny. "Taste and see that the Lord is GOOD" (Ps. 34:8). When we allow Him to motivate us, our motives are right. And that is very important to Him.

Therefore judge nothing before the appointed time; wait till the Lord comes. He will bring to light what is hidden in darkness and will expose the motives of men's hearts. At that time each will receive his praise from God.

1 Corinthians 4:5 NIV

All a man's ways seem innocent to him, but motives are weighed by the Lord.

Proverbs 16:2 NIV

If our motives aren't right—if we're motivated by the wrong things—then the Bible says that our prayers will be affected.

When you ask, you do not receive, because you ask with wrong motives, that you may spend what you get on your pleasures.

James 4:3 NIV

Now it's your turn to encourage others to reach their destiny.

When we're motivated by Him, we'll be more interested in serving others than in being served. Most people underestimate the importance of service. But Jesus didn't. Philippians 2 tells us that Jesus took on the very nature of a servant.

Who, being in very nature God, did not consider equality with God something to be grasped, but made himself nothing, taking the very nature of a servant, being made in human likeness.

Philippians 2:6,7

In fact, He taught us that to be the greatest of all, you must be the servant of all.

Your hands are instruments of service. It's important to get your hands in the mix. If you want to continue to see dreams become destiny in your life, you have to get your hands off your lap and out of your pockets, and start using them in service for God.

Your mouth is another instrument of service. You can become a great encourager. To make it as far as you have on your path to destiny, you were encouraged by someone—maybe a parent, a coach, a trainer, a friend, or a spouse. Now it's your turn to encourage others to reach their destiny.

Sometimes your words will provide the encouragement someone needs to get through the desperation or delays, and sometimes your hands of service will do the encouraging by sharing

Keep something out in front of you that is beyond your grasp and can only be reached with the help of God.

149

someone's load. Either way, you can *never* go wrong by encouraging someone—taking the high road and picking up someone's spirit.

Sometimes it's hard to encourage others because we ourselves need encouragement. God has provided a way for us to stay motivated, and you can find it in Galatians 6:7-9:

> *Don't be misled: No one makes a fool of God. What a person plants, he will harvest. The person who plants self-ishness, ignoring the needs of others—ignoring God!—harvests a crop of weeds. All he'll have to show for his life is weeds! But the one who plants in response to God, letting God's Spirit do the growth work in him, harvests a crop of real life, eternal life.*
>
> *So let's not allow ourselves to get fatigued doing good. At the right time we will harvest a good crop if we don't give up, or quit.*

Keep something out in front of you that is beyond your grasp and can only be reached with the help of God. This will motivate you to pursue Him and continually move closer to His ultimate destiny for you. Then you will walk with Him until you have finished the race, won the prize, and fulfilled every dream He has planted in you.

A NEW DREAM FOLLOWS
THE STADIUM DREAM

After the concert was over and the people were getting ready to leave, the press wanted pictures and quotes for their articles. I'd been blessed to be a part of history. I was privileged to partner with a man of God who'd pursued the dream in his heart because he believed that with God nothing was impossible. (Mark 10:27.)

This night was the entrance into the next season of my life and ministry. This history-making concert had not only inspired and exhausted me; it had changed my life. The next several months of tour, I was prayerful and thoughtful about future things. I'd been so comfortable at Carman Ministries that I'd never thought of doing anything else, but my spirit was restless. I couldn't understand how I could feel this way with everything working so smoothly, but I was feeling something from the inside out. God was ready for me to roll on.

The comfort of a consistent paycheck, and of doing something I'd grown to know so well, kept me at Carman Ministries for five more years before I would obey God and go. Though I was seeing tremendous things happening through the ministry of Carman, I longed for a more personal role. I wanted to touch people through what God was doing *in me.* I desired to see others find their purpose for existence and turn their dreams to destiny, too.

Though Carman Ministries produced several stadium events on the next tour, none of them felt like Texas. To this day, the picture of Texas Stadium hangs on the wall in my study as an igniter to my spirit anytime someone tells me that a project is too big or too expensive. One glance and I'm inspired all over again to pursue excellence and win souls to Jesus.

Jesus said:

The thief does not come except to steal, and to kill, and to destroy. I have come that they may have life, and that they may have it more abundantly.

John 10:10

_____

Jesus provides an abundant life: not just a full life, a FULL-filled life as we do what we are purposed to do. I discovered that there is a difference between being full and being fulfilled. After nearly twenty years with Carman and his ministry, I said good-bye to the field of experience that had taught me how to step out on nothing and find a place to stand. I left filled with hope that I would find my own personal fulfillment in doing what Christ was calling me to do: to be a pastor, to shepherd a flock of His sheep.

Everything I'd experienced at Carman Ministries had been training for this moment. I would leave a comfortable living and a nice home to pursue a passion that I'd barely even dabbled in before.

I made an agreement with God to preach or teach wherever He wanted me to go, and I did it. No matter how big or small the group, I was ready. In my five-year battle with obeying the inner leading of God, it had been as if I were in halftime. Now halftime was over, and I was ready to play!

I began preaching and teaching almost immediately after my departure from Carman Ministries, just as I'd told the Lord I would. He moved my family back to Tulsa, Oklahoma, where my relationship with Carman had begun. There I created and produced a television series called *Dreams2Destiny*, in which I interviewed several popular people from our area, asking each of them which season they were in and how they were moving toward their destiny. I was even editing the show in the office Carman and I had built for ministry.

But God had even more in store for me. With the television series, God was propelling me to begin a church.

Okay, God, I questioned, *You want me to build and pastor a church in a city that has churches everywhere? Why? Tulsa doesn't need another church!*

Though we endure seasons of desperation and delay, we have the divine assurance that God will do in us what He says He will do

Then the Lord responded, letting me know that Tulsa not only needed another church, but it needed our church: a place where people from all faith backgrounds could come and land in an environment where they could experience Christ. A place where those who had been bruised and battered by churches, believers, and ministries could come back and be healed, strengthened, and set apart for service once again.

For two more years, I was in a holding pattern, waiting for the right time and the right place to land. I was waiting for God to show me a bit more of the puzzle.

Then, in March of 2002, we began The Landing Community Church in Tulsa. It would be a safe place for those who found themselves in a "spiritual holding pattern" to land and be themselves while God ignited their dreams. There they could pursue their destiny with the help of others who truly cared about them and the dream God had planted in them.

So now I have found my way into another God-given dream, and the cycle of seasons continues as the church moves forward. Though we endure seasons of desperation and delay, we have the divine assurance that God will do in us what He says He will do, and our destiny is certain to happen in our future.

I have learned that as you help build great people, you help build a great church. I've learned to read the signs and pay attention to the seasons. All I must do is move through the seasons to turn my dreams to destiny. I've seen it happen before. I've watched history. I've even been part of it. That makes it easier for me to get through the changing seasons now.

Now that you have become acquainted with the five seasons on the journey from dreams to destiny, what will you do? How much do you desire to see your potential and purpose realized? As you learn through experience more about the seasons, you will learn daily how to navigate through them and fulfill dream after dream. Then one day you will find your way to the very destiny God had in mind for you when He breathed life into your body. And there is no better place to be!

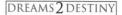
EVALUATING YOUR JOURNEY

A New Dream Begins

Start praying today for God to make His dreams for you real. It's okay to just take little steps toward fulfilling them, as long as you keep moving forward. Today you can start turning dreams to destiny. Remember: with God all things are possible! (Mark 10:27.)

As you seek the Lord and His will for your life, He will guide you on your journey. As you commit to Him, He'll start to plant new desires in your heart that He'll help you fulfill. He'll speak to you as you listen for that still, small voice. (1 Kings 19:12.) Then, one miraculous day, you will begin to realize that your dreams are becoming your destiny. You'll rejoice with the Lord and find your fullness of joy in His presence. You'll see that your dreams have become your destiny!

What dreams have become destiny for you?

_____

_____

_____

_____

_____

_____

_____

_____

_____

_____

_____

_____

_____

_____

_____

_____

_____

_____

_____

God honors those who move out of the pew and into the community, from their seats to the streets to "shake things up" for Him. How can you serve Him by serving others?

_____

_____

_____

_____

_____

_____

_____

_____

_____

_____

_____

_____

What new dreams are you going to pursue?

_____

_____

_____

_____

_____

_____

_____

_____

_____

_____

_____

_____

_____

_____

_____

What Scriptures support your new dreams?

_____

_____

_____

_____

_____

_____

_____

_____

_____

_____

_____

_____

_____

_____

_____

_____

_____

How will your new dreams become your destiny? List five new short-term goals.

_____

_____

_____

_____

_____

_____

_____

_____

_____

_____

_____

_____

_____

_____

DREAMS 2 DESTINY

List five new long-term goals.

_____

_____

_____

_____

_____

_____

_____

_____

_____

_____

_____

_____

_____

_____

_____

162

Journal your thoughts about new dreams.

_____

_____

_____

_____

_____

_____

_____

_____

_____

_____

_____

_____

_____

_____

ENDNOTES

[1] Merriam-Webster Online Dictionary copyright © 2005 by Merriam-Webster, Incorporated, s.v. "dream."

[2] Helen Keller, *Winning Words of Champions,* <http://www.appleseeds.org/Nov_02.htm>.

[3] http://en.thinkexist.com/quotation/nothing_in_this_world_can_take_the_place_of/201002.html.

[4] http://www.painterskeys.com/auth_search.asp?name=Johann+Wolfgang+von+Goethe.

[5] http://www.ordinarypeoplecanwin.com/louholtz.htm.

[6] http://www.quotationspage.com/quote/1574.html.

[7] http://en.thinkexist.com/quotes/Herm_Albright/

PRAYER OF SALVATION

God loves you—no matter who you are, no matter what your past. God loves you so much that He gave His one and only begotten Son for you. The Bible tells us, "...whoever believes in him shall not perish but have eternal life" (John 3:16 NIV). Jesus laid down His life and rose again so that we could spend eternity with Him in heaven and experience His absolute best on earth. If you would like to receive Jesus into your life, say the following prayer out loud and mean it from your heart.

Heavenly Father, I come to You admitting that I am a sinner. Right now, I choose to turn away from sin, and I ask You to cleanse me of all unrighteousness. I believe that Your Son, Jesus, died on the cross to take away my sins. I also believe that He rose again from the dead so that I might be forgiven of my sins and made righteous through faith in Him. I call upon the name of Jesus Christ to be the Savior and Lord of my life. Jesus, I choose to follow You and ask that You fill me with the power of the Holy Spirit. Give me your dream for my life, and use that dream to fulfill the destiny You created for me. I am saved in Jesus' name. Amen.

If you prayed this prayer to receive Jesus Christ as your Savior for the first time, please contact us on the Web at **www.harrisonhouse.com** to receive a free book.

Or you may write to us at

Harrison House
P.O. Box 35035
Tulsa, Oklahoma 74153

ABOUT THE AUTHOR

Joseph S. Jones has devoted his life and abilities to helping others move dreams2destiny. He is the founder of Dreams2Destiny Center, Inc., a nonprofit organization that helps people discover their life purpose and move toward the fulfillment of that purpose. As a life coach, Joe helps many people get back on track and find true meaning for their lives and a place for their talents.

Using his talents for incorporating ministry in business and business in ministry, Joe has been instrumental in fashioning the careers of many musicians and ministries. From 1985 until March of 2000, he directed Carman Ministries as its vice president and executive director. His experience has afforded him the opportunity to participate in extraordinary works for Christ, domestic and abroad, including the production of the history making Texas Stadium event, as well as the largest ticketed concert in Johannesburg, South Africa, both with Carman Ministries.

In 2000, Joe resigned from Carman Ministries to pursue a calling to minister and teach God's Word, and to help ministries and organizations "enlarge the place of their tent" (Isaiah 54:2). His experiences have given him great insight into thinking outside of the natural and developing the SUPER-natural in business and in ministry.

In March of 2002, he began The Landing Community Church in Tulsa, Oklahoma. As founding senior pastor, Joe guides those entrusted to his care and creates and environment where people can uncover their purpose, broaden their influence, and reach their destiny.

Joe has authored two other books, titled *Don't Quit* and *Fatal Affliction,* and he writes a monthly Internet column called "Cup of Joe."

You may contact Joseph Jones by writing

8303-J East 111 Street South

Bixby, Oklahoma 74008

or calling 918-369-8777

www.thelandingonline.com

email: thelanding@olp.net

*Please include your prayer requests
and praise reports when you write.*

www.harrisonhouse.com

Fast. Easy. Convenient!

- ◆ New Book Information
- ◆ Look Inside the Book
- ◆ Press Releases
- ◆ Bestsellers
- ◆ Free E-News
- ◆ Author Biographies

- ◆ Upcoming Books
- ◆ Share Your Testimony
- ◆ Online Product Availability
- ◆ Product Specials
- ◆ Order Online

For the latest in book news and author information, please visit us on the Web at www.harrisonhouse.com. Get up-to-date pictures and details on all our powerful and life-changing products. Sign up for our e-mail newsletter, *Friends of the House,* and receive free monthly information on our authors and products including testimonials, author announcements, and more!

Harrison House—
Books That Bring Hope, Books That Bring Change

THE HARRISON HOUSE VISION

Proclaiming the truth and the power

Of the Gospel of Jesus Christ

With excellence;

Challenging Christians to

Live victoriously,

Grow spiritually,

Know God intimately.